TWAYNE'S WORLD AUTHORS SERIES

A Survey of the World's Literature

FRANCE

Maxwell A. Smith, Guerry Professor of French, Emeritus
The University of Chattanooga
Former Visiting Professor in Modern Languages
The Florida State University

EDITOR

Charles Péguy

TWAS 467

Charles Péguy

CHARLES PÉGUY

By F. C. ST. AUBYN

University of Pittsburgh

TWAYNE PUBLISHERS

A DIVISION OF G. K. HALL & CO., BOSTON

Copyright © 1977 by G. K. Hall & Co.

All Rights Reserved

First Printing

Library of Congress Cataloging in Publication Data

St. Aubyn, Frederic Chase, 1921–
    Charles Péguy.

    (Twayne's world authors series ; TWAS 467 : France.
    Bibliography: pp. 157–70.
    Includes index
    1. Péguy, Charles Pierre, 1873–1914—Criticism and in-
terpretation.
PQ2631.E25Z775   848'.9'1209   77-5948
ISBN 0-8057-6304-X

For Bob and Katie

Contents

About the Author

Preface

Chronology

1. Overture: Poet and Peasant 15

2. The Socialist Pamphleteer: 1897–1902 25

3. The Socialist Pamphleteer: 1903–1907 42

4. The Catholic Pamphleteer: 1909–1910 58

5. The Catholic Pamphleteer: 1910–1914 74

6. The Poet: 1897–1912 88

7. The Poet: 1913 104

8. The Theme of Absence 118

9. The Literary Critic 126

10. Conclusion: An Eternal Flame 145

Notes and References 153

Selected Bibliography 157

Index 171

About the Author

F. C. St. Aubyn received his B.A. from Southwest Missouri State University and the M.A. and Ph.D. from Yale University. After teaching at Harpur College, the University of Delaware, and Elmira College, he went to the University of Pittsburgh where he is presently Professor of French in the Department of French and Italian. Dr. St. Aubyn is the author of the Twayne's World Authors Series volumes on *Stéphane Mallarmé* (1969) and *Arthur Rimbaud* (1975). In addition to co-editing two textbooks, his articles on modern French literature have appeared in England, France, and Italy, as well as the United States. He was the recipient of a Fellowship from the American Council of Learned Societies in 1967–1968.

Preface

This book is intended to serve as a general introduction to the works of Péguy in prose and poetry for students and teachers in high schools, colleges, and universities, as well as for the general public. No attempt has been made to prove a thesis of any kind. The desire was to analyze as faithfully as possible what Péguy said in all those thousands of lines of prose and poetry in order to come to some conclusion about his contributions to French literature and life.

I have included a chronology, a brief biography, an analysis of the major works, an estimate of the importance of Péguy's place in French literature and of his influence on that literature, as well as a selected bibliography, all of which I hope will help the student in approaching Péguy's works. As with most writers and their readers, the relationship must be a personal one. Some may find less in Péguy than I did, but many will find much more.

I should like to thank Professors Maxwell A. Smith and Sylvia E. Bowman for providing me with this opportunity to stretch my horizons and increase my knowledge, two never-ending but very pleasant tasks.

F. C. St. Aubyn

University of Pittsburgh

Chronology

1873 January 7: Birth of Charles-Pierre Péguy at Orleans, son of Désiré Péguy, carpenter, and Cécile Quéré Péguy, chairmender. November 18: Death of Péguy's father. He is raised by his mother and grandmother.

1885 Easter: Awarded a municipal scholarship. Péguy enters the lycée.

1887 February 12: Maternal grandmother, Etiennette Quéré, dies.

1891 July 21: Receives his bachelor's degree in letters. October: Enters the Lycée Lakanal at Sceaux on a state scholarship. Ceases to practice the Catholic religion.

1892 June 17–22: Passes the written examination for entrance into the École Normale Supérieure but fails the oral and loses his scholarship. November 11: Enlists in the 131st Infantry Regiment at Orleans.

1893 September 28: Completes his military service. October: Enters the Collège Sainte-Barbe in the heart of the Latin Quarter in Paris on a scholarship.

1894 August 9–16: Travels to Orange to see Mounet-Sully in Sophocles' *OEdipus the King*. October: Receives the bachelor's degree in sciences and the *licence* in letters (philosophy). November 2: Enters the École Normale. December 19–22: Courtmartial of Dreyfus.

1895 April: "Officially" becomes a Socialist. November 2–4: Visits Domremy and Vaucouleurs, the home of Joan of Arc. November 30: Obtains a year's leave of absence from the École Normale and returns to Orleans to work on *Jeanne d'Arc*.

1896 July 25: His closest friend, Marcel Baudouin, dies in Paris. October 21: Receives permission to repeat the second year at the École Normale to which he returns in November.

1897   February: Publishes his first article, "Un économiste socialiste: M. Léon Walras," in *La Revue socialiste*. October 28: Marries Charlotte-Françoise Baudouin, sister of his late friend Marcel. December: Publishes *Jeanne d'Arc*.

1898   May 1: Opens a Socialist bookstore. August: Fails the examination for the *agrégation* in philosophy. September 10: Birth of first son, Marcel.

1899   September: To avoid bankruptcy the bookstore is transformed into a cooperative. December 3–8: First national congress of French Socialist organizations. Péguy refuses its control of the press. December 26: Breaks with the cooperative bookstore.

1900   January 5: Founds the *Cahiers de la Quinzaine*. August 27–September 19: Takes part in military maneuvers in the Beauce.

1901   September 7: Birth of Péguy's daughter, Germaine.

1902   August 25–September 25: Attends military school at Coulommiers.

1903   March 24: Publishes *La Chanson du roi Dagobert*. June 16: Birth of second son, Pierre.

1904   August 1–28: Does his military service.

1905   September 9: Promoted lieutenant in the 276th Infantry Regiment.

1908   September 10: Confides to Joseph Lotte that he has returned to the Catholic faith.

1909   April 28–May 9: Does military service at Coulommiers. June 16: Registers his thesis subject with the Sorbonne.

1910   January 16: Publishes *Le Mystère de la charité de Jeanne d'Arc*.

1911   April 25: Publishes his *OEuvres choisies 1900–1910*. June 2: Fails to receive the French Academy prize for literature but is awarded a consolation prize. October 22: Publishes *Le Porche du mystère de la deuxième vertu*.

1912   March 24: Publishes *Le Mystère des saints Innocents*. June 14–17: Makes a pilgrimage on foot to Chartres. November 10: Publishes his "Sonnets" in *Le Correspon-*

dant. December 1: Publishes *La Tapisserie de sainte Geneviève et de Jeanne d'Arc.*

1913   May 11: Publishes *La Tapisserie de Notre Dame.* July 25–28: Makes a second pilgrimage to Chartres. December 28: Publishes *Eve.*

1914   August 1: General mobilization. August 2: Takes leave of his family and goes to Paris to bid his friends goodby. August 4: Takes command of a troop train that goes first to Coulommiers. August 10–28: Campaign in Lorraine. Retreat from Montdidier. September 5: Killed by a bullet in the forehead near Villeroy, less than fifteen miles from Paris.

*1915   February 4: Birth of third son, Charles-Pierre.

* The Chronology is based on *OP*, pp. xxix-xli, and Etienne Dennery *et al.*, *Charles Péguy*, pp. xi-xvi.

CHAPTER 1

Overture: Poet and Peasant

PÉGUY was undoubtedly not quite the peasant he liked to believe himself to be. He certainly never tilled the soil and his mother, while not precisely a small landowner, did at one time possess three houses in the suburb of Orleans where Péguy was born. Any man who fulfills all the requirements for the highest academic degree in France except passing the comprehensive examinations and defending his thesis, has forever removed himself from the comparatively uneducated peasant class. Thus Péguy quite honestly subtitles his autobiography, published posthumously, "The Beginnings of a Bourgeois Life."[1]

Péguy was nevertheless of peasant origin at least on his mother's side. His maternal grandmother, who could not read, was the first to teach him the French language, as Péguy liked to claim.[2] Born on January 7, 1873, Péguy was the only son of Désiré Péguy, a carpenter by trade, and Cécile Quéré Péguy, a chairmender. Péguy never knew his father who died slightly more than ten months after the birth of his son from the hardships suffered during the siege of Paris in the Franco-Prussian War. Péguy himself died in the defense of Paris just four months before the birth of his third son.

Péguy's childhood was filled with hard work since his mother, his grandmother, and the little boy each had to complete assigned tasks in order to prevent the fatherless household from foundering economically. He entered primary school in 1879. When he graduated in 1884, he was enrolled in a professional school or what we would call a trade school. But Péguy's scholastic aptitude had already been noted by the head of the primary school who secured for him a full municipal scholarship at the Lycée d'Orléans so that he might continue his academic studies. He received his French baccalaureate in 1891 when, with the aid of a state scholarship, he entered the Lycée Lakanal in the little town of Sceaux just south of Paris. Sometime during his year at Sceaux Péguy ceased to practice the Catholic religion—to which he would return seventeen years later.

I *The Student*

In 1892 Péguy passed the written examinations for entrance into the École Normale Supérieure but failed the orals and lost his scholarship. This academic failure was the first of several that Péguy would suffer, a fact that might help to explain his later splenetic attacks upon the professors of the Sorbonne. He returned to Orleans and enlisted in the 131st Infantry Regiment. When one notes how extensive Péguy's literary creation was, one is impressed by the amount of time he spent in the military. After completing his service in 1893 he entered the Collège Sainte-Barbe in the heart of the Latin Quarter in Paris to prepare again for the École Normale. Péguy lived in central Paris only for the two years he was a student. The rest of his adult life he lived in what can only be described as the distant suburbs of Paris, although he was to spend all his working life in the Latin Quarter on the Left Bank almost literally in the shadow of the Sorbonne. The following year he failed the examination for the *licence* but succeeded in gaining entrance to the École Normale.

In the summer of that year he traveled to the great Roman theater at Orange in the south of France to see the renowned actor Mounet-Sully perform in Sophocles' *OEdipus the King*. His classical studies, reinforced by this impressive performance, helped form Péguy's literary taste and style. Péguy never crossed the frontiers of France so that this trip to Orange was the longest he ever made. That fall Péguy received his bachelor's degree in sciences at the École Normale. He had hardly begun his studies again when Captain Dreyfus was courtmartialed from December 19 to 22, an event that shaped Péguy's life forever.

II *The Dreyfusite*

In the spring of 1895 he declared himself "officially" a Socialist. Just what, aside from his reading, influenced him to do this is still not completely clear. Early in November he visited Domremy, the birthplace of Joan of Arc in western France. That same month, after all his tribulations in gaining entrance, Péguy applied for and received a year's leave of absence from his studies. He returned to Orleans, this time to learn typography, to help organize a section of the Socialist party, and to work on his *Jeanne d'Arc* (Joan of Arc), a project he had evidently begun at least two years earlier at Sainte-Barbe. The following year his best friend, Marcel Baudouin, died in Paris. The relationship, evidently based on a mutually shared view of life and politics, was close enough to cause Péguy to sign his earliest works with the pseudonym Pierre Baudouin and to credit Marcel with help in the writing of, or at least in the inspiration for *Jeanne d'Arc*. Péguy married Baudouin's sister Charlotte in 1897. They named their first son Marcel. A man by the name of Victor Boudon was with Péguy when the latter was killed in the early days of World War I. Coincidences like Baudouin-Boudon seem to haunt Péguy's life.

Before his marriage Péguy received permission to repeat his second year at the École Normale in 1896. Early in 1897 at the age of twenty-four he published his first article on the Socialist economist, Léon Walras, married Charlotte in October, and published *Jeanne d'Arc* in December. One copy of the play was sold.

In 1898, Péguy became more actively involved in French politics. While Dreyfus was languishing in prison on Devil's Island in French Guiana, Dreyfus's family and others had not ceased their efforts to prove his innocence. Bit by bit the truth leaked out that this Jewish captain on the General Staff had been unjustly condemned on what was at first an erroneous interpretation of very meager circumstantial evidence. Later, to protect the "honor" of the Army, the evidence was tampered with, an attempt too ludicrous to be believed. Finally Zola could contain himself no longer. He burst forth with his famous article "J'accuse!" in January, 1898, and the battle was on. Zola was forced to seek refuge in England, while the Latin Quarter of 1898 must have been much like that of 1968 with invasions and counter-invasions and skirmishes between the Dreyfusites and the anti-Dreyfusites. Péguy was in the thick of this conflict,

defending physically the cause of justice about which he felt
so strongly spiritually, morally, and emotionally. This crisis of
the French conscience during the Third Republic did not end
until eight year later in 1906 with the military ceremony that
restored to Dreyfus his public honor, his civil rights, and his
military rank. Many years more were necessary before France
recovered from the effects of this tragic affair, if she ever did.
Certainly a large part of Péguy's life was caught up in this
turmoil that would color everything he would write in future
years.

III   *The Bookstore Manager*

The year 1898 was eventful for Péguy in many other ways.
His wife's family were ardent Socialists and readily concurred
in his using his wife's modest inheritance to found a Socialist
bookstore. Since Péguy was a scholarship student, he could not
legally own and operate a business so the firm was given the
name of Péguy's friend Georges Bellais. In August Péguy failed
the notoriously difficult examination for the *agrégation* in philosophy. This was his last attempt to enter the academic world
aside from his somewhat pointless gesture of registering a thesis
topic with the Sorbonne in 1909. In the fall of 1898 his first son,
Marcel, was born.

Hardly more than a year of monumental mismanagement on
the part of the inexperienced and inept Péguy and his friends
was necessary to bring the bookstore to the brink of bankruptcy.
To salvage as much as possible the bookstore was transformed
in September into a cooperative with the somewhat cumbersome
name of the Société Nouvelle de librairie et d'édition (New
Bookstore and Publishing Society). The board of directors, so
to speak, of the cooperative with Péguy as publisher was varied.
It included among others the librarian of the École Normale,
Lucien Herr, who exerted an enormous intellectual and political
influence in the Latin Quarter; Mario Roque, a famous philologist and professor at the Collège de France; and the Socialist
politician and writer, Léon Blum, who was to play an important
role in French politics for fifty years to come.

Early in December of 1899 the first national congress of French

Socialist organizations was held. To his dismay Péguy discovered that the central committee had no intention of allowing anyone and everyone to publish anything and everything he might like about party politics. Péguy rightfully felt that the revelation and admission of error, constructive criticism, and the expression of a multiplicity of views were more important than prefabricated and rigidly controlled political propaganda. He broke with the central committee and thus with the party while remaining a convinced Socialist. To his even greater dismay Péguy learned late in the same month that the directors of the cooperative also had no intention of allowing him to publish anything he desired. He immediately broke with the Société. Thus Péguy found himself at the eve of the new year and the turn of the century a man without a religion, without a party, and without a publishing house.

IV *The Editor*

Péguy reacted quickly and decisively. By January 5, 1900, he had founded and published the first issue of the *Cahiers de la Quinzaine* (*Bimonthly Notebooks*). His editorial policy was idealistic. No advertising was to be accepted for fear of inhibiting the freedom of expression. Those interested in the review would support it financially according to a sliding scale of ability to pay. All points of view were welcome. No manuscript would be censored although the author might later find himself the object of a strongly worded rebuttal if his ideas differed from those of Péguy. All literary forms, poetry, plays, novels, short stories, essays, and historical documents were acceptable.

For the first ten years Péguy published, aside from his essays, only one collection of his own poems, *La Chanson du roi Dagobert* (*The Song of King Dagobert*), in 1903. Otherwise the roster of authors read like a list of the famous men of the time: Maurice Barrès, Julien Benda, Anatole France, Daniel Halévy, Jean Jaurès, François Porché, Romain Rolland, André Suarès, Jérôme and Jean Tharaud, to mention only a few. The works of Romain Rolland, his *Life of Beethoven* and his long novel *Jean-Christophe*, for example, were the financial mainstay of the *Cahiers*. In spite of Péguy's heroic efforts one must admit that almost all the authors he published are not much read today. The essayists are read by historians and by political and social scientists because of their influence upon French life and the thought of the period. The poets and novelists are read as a necessary part of literary history but hardly for their literary merit. No Gide, no Proust, no Apollinaire found his way into the *Cahiers*. Only in 1910 when Péguy began to publish his *Mystères* (*Mysteries*) and his *Tapisseries* (*Tapestries*) did the *Cahiers* assume an enduring literary significance, and some critics would dispute even that claim to fame.

The list of Péguy's essays published and unpublished during his lifetime runs into the dozens. Péguy had already published two utopian essays, the first in 1897 in *La Revue socialiste* (*The Socialist Review*), the second the following year as editor of the Georges Bellais Bookstore. In the first issue of the *Cahiers* he began his campaign against censorship by the Socialist party, in the fourth against parliamentary government and majority rule. Also in 1900 Péguy made the first of a series of attacks on Jean Juarès that would eventually alienate the two friends. In September Péguy took part in military maneuvers in the Beauce, a region to which he would return twice in a dramatic way. The Dreyfus Affair was far from forgotten. Péguy explained that he could not write the history of Dreyfusism in France because the spirit of the movement was all but dead, an instance in which Péguy was both right and wrong. In repeating the utopian manifesto that he had already drawn up for the publication which he had hoped to edit earlier, Péguy revealed both his ideals where the *Cahiers* were concerned and the role the Dreyfus Affair had already played in his life. The break with the Société still rankled Péguy to the extent that early in 1901 he published an essay in which he excoriated Lucien Herr for his part in the breach. This essay was his first attack on a member of the university community and eventually led to a condemnation of many professors. Thus in one year most of the major themes of Péguy's subsequent essays had been established. Péguy's only daughter Germaine was born in September 1901. One must continually remind oneself that Péguy had a family living in the suburbs of Paris because they appear only much later in his writings.

In 1902 almost everyone including Péguy had intimations that the Dreyfus case would be reopened. Thus for the next four years the Affair frequently occupied his attention. As a student Péguy had encountered Blanche Raphaël. By 1902 the whole family—father, son, and daughter—were aiding the *Cahiers* financially and in other ways. Blanche later had a great influence on Péguy's emotional life and consequently on his poetry. Péguy published a group of amusing little poems, *La Chanson du roi Dagobert*, his first poetry since *Jeanne d'Arc*, in 1903, the same year his second son Pierre was born. In his essays he continued his fight against anti-clericalism and what he called modern times which he dated from about 1880.

The events of 1905 radically changed Péguy's way of think-ing. The year began with the slaughter of the Russian people in the square before the Winter Palace who had only come peacefully to beg the aid of their tsar. That same year an attempt was made to assassinate the king of Spain during a state visit in Paris. Then, the German kaiser, William II, could not resist defying both England and France by landing in Morocco and parading proudly through the streets of Tangiers. In this act, he threatened the balance of power that the two countries were trying to maintain in North Africa. One can thus say that both the Russian Revolution and World War I had their beginnings in 1905. From that time on Péguy's patriotism became super-patriotism. He not only began to foretell World War I but also, in a way, to foreordain his own death.

Péguy continued his tirades against the excesses of the modern world until October 1907. While recovering from a serious ill-ness in the autumn of 1908 Péguy revealed his return to the Catholic faith to his friend Joseph Lotte. The revelation did not mean a return to the church but it did occasion much anguish for both Péguy and his family who remained staunch Socialists. The Catholic philosopher Jacques Maritain attempted to inter-vene between Péguy and his wife and mother-in-law with disastrous results. The religious rift in the Péguy household was not healed until after Péguy's death with the conversion of Madame Péguy and their children.

Although Péguy had by this time alienated many of his old friends he did find pleasure in the company of the wealthy son of a former president of France, Claude Casimir-Périer, and more particularly his wife. They invited him to spend restful weekends at their chateau Trie-en-Ville. Madame Péguy was conspicuous by her absence. Claude had been on maneuvers with Péguy. His wife Simone was both an actress and a cousin of Péguy's friend Julien Benda. Péguy also made the acquaintance of Henri Alain-Fournier who replaced Jaurès as a walking companion in the countryside near Péguy's suburban home. Fournier published his splendid novel *Le Grand Meaulnes* (*The Great Meaulnes*) in 1913 and disappeared forever in World War I on September 22, 1914, just seventeen days after the death of Péguy.

V   *The Poet*

Péguy began to publish again in the *Cahiers* in June 1909 with a plea for money for his almost bankrupt review. Early in 1910 his first mystery, *Le Mystère de la charité de Jeanne d'Arc* (*The Mystery of the Charity of Joan of Arc*), appeared. During the years 1910–1913 Péguy published feverishly. He was thus, without quite realizing it perhaps, asking his subscribers to subsidize his own publications. By 1910 Péguy's deep passion for Blanche Raphaël was causing him great agony. She was safely married that year while Péguy remained faithful to his wife and family. He evidently never recovered, however, from his infatuation which expressed itself partially between 1910 and 1912 in his endless *Quatrains* published in 1939 and *La Ballade du coeur* (*The Ballad of the Heart*) that appeared in 1973. The year 1911 was traumatic for Péguy in quite a different way. He hoped to obtain the Grand Prize for Literature from the French Academy which carried an award of ten thousand francs. To that end and to increase his visibility on the literary scene, Péguy secured the publication of his *OEuvres choisies 1900–1910* (*Selected Works 1900–1910*) by Bernard Grasset. By a fluke Péguy's old friend Romain Rolland along with others appeared on the Academy's ballot. After several inconclusive votes the Academy decided not to award the prize that year but gave Péguy consolation in the form of the Estrade Delcros Prize worth eight thousand francs. Péguy was not consoled.

Nor was 1912 an easy year for Péguy. His son Pierre contracted typhoid and fell seriously ill. Péguy vowed to make a pilgrimage to Chartres if his son was spared. When his son recovered, Péguy walked to Chartres June 14–17, crossing again the lovely land of the Beauce he had seen earlier while on military maneuvers. He made a second pilgrimage to Chartres the following year and thus began the tradition of the pilgrimage on foot from Paris to Chartres undertaken so often ever since by thousands of the faithful. Péguy published *Le Mystère des saints Innocents* (*The Mystery of the Holy Innocents*) and *La Tapisserie de sainte Geneviève et de Jeanne d'Arc* (*The Tapestry of St. Genevieve and Joan of Arc*) in 1912 as well as his "Sonnets" which were hardly the traditional fourteen-line poem. In 1913 he published a second *Tapisserie* (*Tapestry*) and his *Eve* in addition to some of his most significant essays.

Péguy ably defended the philosopher Henri Bergson in 1914 against condemnation by the Catholic church, but in June the assassination in Sarajevo took place and World War I became inevitable. When general mobilization was called on August 1 Péguy, rather than spending his last days and hours with his family or making the trip to Orleans to see his mother, went to Paris August 2 to say goodby to his friends and perhaps to reconcile some differences with them. That he dropped his pen in mid-sentence upon hearing the call to arms I find unbelievably dramatic.

Nevertheless, the embattled and embittered pamphleteer continued his brave struggle in war as he had in peace. That he was unconsciously and probably even consciously seeking death does not detract from his heroic determination. The heritage he left us consists of literally thousands of pages. More than sixty years after his death readers, critics, and scholars are still trying to separate the grain from the chaff. Some regret the ambiguity of his works that made it possible for them to be used and ill-used by both the Resistance and the Vichy regime during World War II. Others are busy building unholy chapels, making an idol of a man who would have been the first to react violently against such canonization. Péguy was both a petty man and a generous man, at times a great writer and more often a bad writer. Those who bless all of his works without reservation have undoubtedly done as much harm as those who reject them out of hand. Only a close look at the major works can help us to decide whether Péguy's significance is transient or enduring.

CHAPTER 2

The Socialist Pamphleteer: 1897–1902

PÉGUY was an impressive pamphleteer. He lacked the one talent that would have made him a great pamphleteer: brevity. Nowhere is this fact better demonstrated than by Péguy himself in his early essays. Disenchanted with Catholicism and attracted to Socialism, Péguy rapidly became an ardent supporter of the cause, always in his own way.

I *The Socialist Utopia*

Among his first articles is one entitled "De la cité socialiste" (Concerning the Socialist City)[1] published in 1897 under the pseudonym Pierre Deloire, a clear and succinct statement of Socialist goals. The one unsettling point in his program, which Péguy discusses extensively, is the necessity of forced labor to ensure that the boring and painful jobs get done. This plan is preferable, Péguy maintains, to the present method which constrains certain members of society to perform odious tasks. One utopian dream that has not, after more than seventy-five years, become a reality is the three or four hour work day. With the exception of this section, Péguy says what he has to in the fewest words possible.

The moment Péguy leaves the practical for the theoretical he immediately loses all sense of proportion. In 1898 he published "Marcel, premier dialogue de la cité harmonieuse" (Marcel, First Dialogue on the Harmonious City, pp. 9–86), dedicated to his dead friend Marcel Baudouin. In high-flown and stilted style he describes all the attributes of the citizens of this future utopia, forgetting the important axiom he had laid down in his earlier essay—that is, that humanity in its infinite variety cannot be organized according to an exact scientific method. Like Rimbaud in his Seer Letters, Péguy insists that man is respon-

25

sible for animals and thus includes them in his Socialist society as adolescents. Woman's place is, according to tradition, in the home. In this harmonious city art, science, and philosophy become "disinterested work" unnecessary for the material well being of its citizens. Echoing the "Art for art's sake" theory of the Parnassians, Péguy writes that "The work of art is made for itself in the harmonious city, and thus it gives to the citizens the recollection of beauty" (p. 65). In this scheme "[s]cience is the investigation that scholars make of reality offered to the knowledge of the citizens" (p. 70) while "[a] philosophy is a work of art of which knowledge is the subject matter" (p. 80). Neither artists nor philosophers have students while scientists do, a debatable idea at best. Péguy then repeats, as in a Buddhist sermon, all the things that the artist, the seven types of scientists, and the philosopher will not do in accomplishing their "disinterested work." He thus establishes extended repetition as his first sin against successful pamphleteering.

II *Freedom of Censorship*

Péguy was completely successful, however, in setting forth the goals of his publication, the *Cahiers*. In his "Lettre du provincial" (Letter from a Provincial, pp. 87–102) of 1900 he begins his campaign against the dictates of the Socialist party announced at its congress the preceeding year. Borrowing his title from Pascal's "Letters to a Provincial," Péguy makes his first critical remark about the great Socialist leader Jean Jaurès because of the latter's support of the party and thus of its limitation of the freedom of the press. In addition to telling "the truth, the whole truth, and nothing but the truth," Péguy swears to tell "the stupid truth stupidly, the boring truth boringly, and the sad truth sadly" (p. 94). This aim is admirable, however, the truth that Péguy subsequently reveals is, as it perhaps had to be, a personal and highly colored version of the truth.

Péguy could also draw a magnificent verbal picture of a "popular" demonstration that fizzled. In "Le 'Triomphe de la République'" (The "Triumph of the Republic," pp. 103–22) of 1900, he mentions names and causes that are all but forgotten, yet the humor and irony of this grandiose and "unforgettable" manifestation, carefully organized and completely mismanaged, are not lost on the modern reader.

III *Parliamentay Democracy*

One of his earliest and longest essays was published in three parts, "De la grippe" (Concerning the Grippe, pp. 123–38), "Encore de la grippe" (Still Concerning the Grippe, pp. 139–71), and "Toujours de la grippe" (Always Concerning the Grippe, pp. 172–204), in 1900. Again borrowing an idea from Pascal, that of the "Prayer Asking God for the Good Use of Illnesses" Péguy creates a dialogue between a patient and his doctor in which he reveals many of his fundamental ideas and profound prejudices. Still smarting from a remark made by his old friend Lucien Herr when Péguy quit the Société Nouvelle to found the *Cahiers*, Péguy swears never to militate against any individual but only against injustice. (Ironically, although Péguy promotes this ideal in this essay, he could not live up to it. His friends' hostility to his enterprise led him to become personally vindictive at times.) Péguy's former friends had predicted failure for his enterprise and now seemed to be working actively to achieve it. Being ill, Péguy calls for the doctor. The latter is amazed that Péguy has not followed parliamentary procedure in deciding to ask him to come, giving Péguy the opportunity to satirize all the weaknesses of that form of government. Like the Socialist party and its recent decision not to reveal the whole truth, Péguy remarks that doctors do not tell the whole truth to their patients in order not to harm or upset them. Among society's sick the doctor lists "the individual and collective ambitious, the authoritarians, the unitarians, the Boulangists, the competitors, the electrocultivators, and the parliamentarians" (p. 131).

The collective ambitious are the followers of Jules Guesde, the grand old man of French Socialism. They transformed their veneration for Guesde into a syndicate for the young ambitious while the authoritarians are revolutionaries who govern by force rather than by reason. The unitarians prefer to unite by force those who are right with those who are wrong. Boulangism—that is, the party that wanted General Georges Boulanger to attempt to overthrow the government in 1889—had been an epidemic that now threatened to become endemic. The competitors are Socialists who still indulge in or have respect for individual and collective competition while the electrocultivators are Socialists only in order to be elected delegates to the congresses or members of the general committee. The parliamentarians indulge in all the tricks of bourgeois parliament. Such are the politicians who have brought about "the decomposition of Dreyfusism in France" (p. 138), the degeneration of the will to fight for the truth against all odds.

In the second part Péguy blames, ironically, the French Romantics, his "personal enemies," for having discredited work. With their claims to sudden illumination, they have encouraged young Socialists to hope for a swift social revolution when such a revolution can only be realized through slow, meticulous work. This line of thought brings Péguy to Ernest Renan, the man who expressed his "elitist" ideas in his *Philosophical Dialogues* of 1871 and thus helped create "modern" French society with its exclusivism. The founding of "popular universities," what we should call evening classes or adult education, was one attempt to eliminate the pernicious influence of elitism by making education available to all workers who wanted it. Péguy criticizes Jaurès for his revolutionary words about the founding of the universities which spoke louder than Jaurès' recent apparent acquiescence to party censorship. Renan held out a false hope for society just as religion had. If the men of the church had worked a little harder and prayed a little less, society would not be as sick as it is, for, as Péguy says, "to pray is not to work" (p. 157). Witnessing the horrors of French and English colonialism in Africa, Péguy proclaimed that world society is sick. Thus Péguy told a truth that was not acted upon for sixty years. Observing that the sick man thinks of death, Péguy wonders if the true Christian doesn't have a secret desire to die in order to realize salvation. He uses two examples to illustrate his point, that of a rich woman and Pascal. He might well have used himself later as an example.

Péguy concludes by recalling that he had forgotten the details of Pascal's death although he had read the story in preparation for his examinations. He concludes that such scholastic competition is another form of bourgeois competition that should be eliminated because it is ineffectual. The relationship between the humble woman's ideas on death and those of a great man like Pascal, which proved the formidable power of religion, has a significant impact on Péguy. He would like to establish a close relationship between the ideas of the great Socialists and those of the simple citizen. But this end would be impossible to achieve in view of the general committee's censorship decree. According to religion, life on earth is a punishment that may terminate only in "a strange combination of life and death that we call damnation, this strange reinforcement of presence through absence and the reinforcement of all through eternity" (p. 192). This statement, despite frequent and lengthy digressions (perhaps more apparent than real), is Péguy's main point. In this essay Péguy commits his second sin against successful pamphleteering by quoting extensively from Anatole France, Jaurès, Renan, Pascal, Sophocles, Racine, and others. He refuses to reduce his thoughts to "two or three short, awkward, inexact, and false formulas, all the events of our inner life" (p. 189). If one reads Pascal's phrase, "Man is only a thinking reed" (p. 186), one can see that Péguy was often incapable of producing such short, graceful, and precise formulas.

IV *Art and Socialism*

Péguy was irritated that a speech by Jaurès on art and Socialism had appeared simultaneously in two Socialist newspapers. This duplication was unnecessary. In his "Brève réponse à Jaurès" (Brief Reply to Jaurès, pp. 239–81) of 1900, Péguy, in dialogue with himself, quotes so much of Jaurès' speech that his article almost constitutes a third and yet another useless repetition. Péguy wanted cooperation rather than competition among the Socialist publications. He was proud to operate the *Cahiers* without advertising and publicity almost as if the harmonious city already existed, which brings us to his real disagreement with Jaurès. Péguy believed that "great" oratory often proves to be something less than great literature on the printed page. One can be confident, however, that Jaurès's auditors were relieved that he did not harangue them on a subject like the harmonious city. Jaurès was speaking to a live audience, attempting to illustrate the evolution of the role of the artist from the bourgeois to a Socialist society. Péguy objected to Jaurès' desire to give artists "the advantages that bourgeois society conferred on them" (p. 253) in a Socialist society. Such an idea did not conform to Péguy's concept of the role of the artist in his harmonious city, a utopian situation in which the artist would not be in need of recompense because everyone would be free and would receive just recompense after contributing freely to the material well being of the city. According to Péguy there could be no Socialist concept of art, only a human concept.

Jaurès also made the mistake of mentioning the Dreyfus Affair, maintaining that such a jolt to the national conscience would undoubtedly provoke new forms of art. Péguy was furious at the idea that "this frightful drama could supply subject matter for literature" (pp. 246–7). He went so far as to say that "it is immoral to divert the acts of life . . . to the ends of art, just as it is unsuitable to want to subject works of art to the ends of life" (pp. 248–9). To the bourgeois axiom that "genius will out" (p. 253) Péguy opposed again the free development of the artist in his harmonious city. No one was more surprised than Péguy when he actually found himself agreeing with Renan and his *The Future of Science*, but only because Renan had not understood the significance of his own ideas. Renan stated that the thinker does not live by his thoughts but by teaching, the least appropriate livelihood for any creative person. Péguy was also careful, however, to quote some examples of Renan's most outrageous elitist ideas, proving again that Péguy's concept of the role of the artist was the only sound one. Jaurès spoke of the role of the museum in Socialist society and of course Péguy could not agree with that either. He would return all pillaged art to its country of origin so that museums would be filled with works of the people, by the people, and for the people. Péguy concluded his disquisition on the mystique of the museum with the totally unexpected observation, "Recalling my unhappy childhood it seemed to me in effect that, with some honorable exceptions, the people who had raised me had always raised me for themselves" (p. 281).

Péguy's "brief" reply was the beginning of the end of his admiration for Jaurès. In it he insulted another professor of the

Sorbonne, the literary historian Ferdinand Brunetière, referred to Alfred de Vigny as haunted by the story of unhappy artists and poets, wrote somewhat disparagingly of the fame of Zola, Tolstoy, and Hugo, quoted the poem "La Justice" of Sully-Prudhomme in which he found a nascent nationalism, and praised Michelet as a visionary historian. Péguy recognized that justice and patriotism are not always the same thing. In his concluding remark, he suggests that he had not been raised for himself and even less for society, but for his parents. Just as Péguy's lack of psychological insight frequently caused him to misjudge the role of art, science, and philosophy in society, it also caused him to misjudge the role of parents in the life of the child and of society. My reaction to Péguy's essay is exactly that of Péguy after reading Jaurès' speech, "a great impression of sterilely optimistic uncertainty" (p. 241).

Much more forceful and to the point was Péguy's "Demi-réponse à M. Cyprien Lantier" (Half-Reply to Mr. Cyprien Lantier, pp. 282–300), late in 1900. Asked why he had not written his history of the decomposition of Dreyfusism in France, Péguy replied by giving an account of a recent meeting of the general committee of the Socialist party at which a motion against anti-semitism was at last to be voted on. After two hours of oratorical effort, Jaurès failed to move his own clear-cut motion because he feared the vote would divide the party. His inaction left the floor open to the ridiculous machinations of committee members who finally voted to protect only those Jews who had declared allegiance to the party according to a very complicated procedure and who had paid for the privilege. If such was the spirit that prevailed within the party, what was left to be said about the degeneration of Dreyfusism in France at large? In eighteen pages Péguy gave exactly the answer that was needed.

V *My Home*

Péguy's last essay of 1900 was called "Pour ma maison" (For My House, pp. 1248–62). Noting that the press was still subject to bourgeois competition, Péguy wanted to establish a truly Socialist newspaper according to five precepts: (1) everyone working for the paper would be paid the same wage since everyone was working for the same goal; (2) there would be no advertising; (3) articles would be written only by specialists in the field; (4) there would be no embellishment of the facts; (5) the newspaper would be a family one aimed at women and children. Several young people went together to found just such a paper, each subscribing according to his means. The affair did not prosper because everyone was too busy with the Dreyfus Affair. Lacking the courage or perhaps through an excess of humility, Péguy did not found the *Cahiers* at that time, rather he poured his wife's dowry into the Georges Bellais Bookstore. The bookstore also did not flourish because of the Dreyfus Affair. Demonstrations in front of this center of Dreyfusism diverted clients while the Affair itself kept the bookstore staff from tending to their business. In addition, the bookstore was not well managed. One book that promised to be a bestseller, Jaurès' *Socialist Action,* turned out to be a dud, perhaps because the Socialist newspaper *La Petite République* did little to promote it.

Even more disastrous was the split among Dreyfusites that came about just as the Affair was ending. Some of them gathered around Péguy's former friend Lucien Herr and became interested only in action, power, authority, and control, while others were interested only in seeing justice done and in making truth evident. Even Jaurès was seduced by the appearance of power through action and thus brought about the downfall of French Socialism, something of a premature judgment on Péguy's part. According to his analysis then, his publishing efforts were inextricably entwined with the developments of the Dreyfus Affair.

VI *For Myself*

Péguy continued the story in his first essay of 1901 entitled "Pour moi" (For Me, pp. 1263–99). Péguy's friends Pierre Baudouin and Pierre Deloire, both of whom are of course Péguy, have come to wish him a happy new year. In the course of the conversation Péguy describes the painful scene in which the five directors of the Société Nouvelle refuse to permit Péguy to assume the administration of the cooperative or to publish a work he is preparing for which he offers to pay. Péguy then founds his own *Cahiers* in which he freely gives publicity to the

publications of the Société. When Péguy asked Herr if he might
read the minutes of the meeting at which this unanimous decision is reached, Herr defers in such a way as to refuse. Péguy's
essay is an attempt to analyze the factors that cause five good
friends and good Socialists to act the way they have. He can
only wonder if "revolutionary Socialism hasn't been contaminated
through its political army just as the French nation was contaminated through its military army" (p. 1292) as revealed by
the Dreyfus Affair. He then fulminates against rule by majority
as an "immoral and irrational bourgeois law" (p. 1295).

VII   *Daredevil*

Péguy's two friends return only to find him in bed with the
grippe. Thus in "Casse-cou" (Daredevil, pp. 303–37) of 1901,
Pierre Baudouin decides to write a letter to Jaurès because of
an article published in *La Petite République* on "The Philosophy
of [Edouard] Vaillant," a Socialist leader. Péguy quotes the
entire article and while no one but the historian is interested
today in Vaillant's philosophy, Péguy's point by point refutation
reveals again his skill in argumentation. That Péguy may also
have been moved to reply because the anonymous author of
the article mentions the "treasures of talent and passionate
sincerity" utilized by Péguy to prove his thesis that "it suffices
for us, in a sort of moralist anarchy, to arouse, from individual
conscience to individual conscience, the pride of the just and the
true" (pp. 309–10) is unimportant. Without mincing words
Péguy maintains that Vaillant knew that Juarès was "basically a
weak one, a good weak one, that is, one who gives way to the
fear of displeasing his enemies, to the fear of causing them
pain, and a little, to the fear of their authority" (p. 311). These
are strong words to apply to France's most famous and most
popular Socialist. When Jaurès had the nerve to title his book
Socialist History, while everyone, according to Péguy, knew that
history cannot be Socialist but only historical, Péguy was one of
Jaurès' few friends with the courage to cry out *casse-cou* (p. 324).

But just when Péguy has made this point he vitiates its force
by citing still more articles as still further examples. The first has
to do with the reception an abbé received when he came to

present the Catholic point of view on education at a popular
university. He is immedately shown the door, an action of which
La Petite République thoroughly approves. Closing the door to
anyone is an exclusion that Péguy cannot condone, particularly
since it eliminates the possibility of arriving at the whole truth.
A second example is the newspaper's criticism of Ferdinand
Brunetière because he titles his book *Discourse on the History of
Literature* which is too similar to Bossuet's title *Discourse on
Universal History*. Brunetière is thus as guilty of perverting
young French minds with religion as Esterhazy is in revealing
details to Schwarzkoppen in the Dreyfus Affair. The analogy,
according to Péguy and any thinking individual, is of course
totally erroneous. The third example is an article on how to apply
the law against the cassock that is so stupid it does not even
merit comment. The fourth example is an article that reveals
the cynicism of everything that has been published on the
amnesty accorded the army officers involved in the Dreyfus
Affair, an amnesty to which Jaurès had agreed. The fifth article
illustrates the ever rising anti-clericalism within the party.
Thus as early as 1901 Péguy was defending the church on non-
religious grounds, giving a clear indication of the reversal his
thought would undergo in 1908.

VIII   *Defeat by Proxy*

If one reads Péguy long enough one eventually learns the
reasons for his diatribes against others. For example, Péguy
never forgives Léon Blum and Lucien Herr for their role in the
Société Nouvelle affair. He never forgives Jaurès for accepting
the army amnesty, for agreeing to party censorship, and for
failing to support his own motion against anti-semitism. In
"Compte rendu de mandat" (Account Rendered of a Mandate,
pp. 338–76) of 1901, one learns why Péguy inveighed against
majority rule. In a genuinely amusing conversation involving the
two Pierres and Péguy's country cousin Désiré Péguy, Péguy
recounts his early participation in Socialism while still in Orleans. He was a member of the Socialist Studies Group of that
city, a small and one might say peripheral group that elected
Péguy to represent it at the first General Congress of French
Socialist Organizations in Paris in 1899. This little group was a

part of the larger French Workers Party which elected its representative, Lucien Roland.

Péguy could not attend the opening of the Congress so he asked his friend Louis Boitier to present his credentials for him as representative of the studies group. In describing the members of the Congress Péguy did not hesitate to state that "We all know that Guesde and Vaillant turned tail during the [Dreyfus] affair, that they abandoned, as you say, justice and truth" (p. 350). Nor could Péguy forgive Léon Blum for reporting after the Congress that "Socialist unity was on the way" (p. 367) when the Guesdist group had withdrawn from the Congress to pass its own resolutions. But what really shook Péguy was the committee's vote of six to five in favor of Roland as representative from Orleans. That kind of majority rule sent Péguy into a frenzy, particularly since he had been stigmatized as an intellectual because of his education while actually he was doing all sorts of manual labor in producing the *Cahiers.* In contrast, Roland was a typographer and thus a manual laborer although he never did any typesetting. Such bourgeois parliamentary competition could only assure that the delegate who was chosen would support the interests of Orleans against those of all other groups, thus dividing rather than uniting the party. The reader gets the impression that Péguy still did not grasp the enormous difference between nurturing one's personal concept of truth and of the harmonious city in the privacy of one's editorial office and getting such concepts accepted by an unwieldy group of hotheaded individualists. Thus as early as 1901 Péguy seemed to exhibit at least some of the traits of a persecution complex while his "dialogues" tend to reveal some of the characteristics of a split personality.

IX   *History as Memory*

Rather than a "Compte rendu de congrès" (Account of a Congress, pp. 379–97), this essay of 1901 was one of Péguy's earliest expositions of his ideas on history. In it he makes his first reference to Henri Bergson, noting how the philosopher's ideas have altered our concept of memory and the matter of memory itself and thus history. The fundamental problem is that of "the relationship of knowledge to action" (p. 386), for as

Péguy puts it, "critical reason comes after the battle" (p. 396).
Michelet remains the first, the best, and the greatest historian
because he did not observe history, he entered into it. In the
same way, Péguy did not attend the Congress as an observer
but as a participant. Since "history is the memory of humanity"
(p. 394), we must make history with what we have, individual
memory, knowledge dominated by action and thus impure
knowledge. As a result, history "demands, in the beginning, that
memory stand aside and in the end that this gap disappear" (p.
395). Rather than an account of the Congress, Péguy gives his
readers a perceptive definition of history, a subject to which he
will return frequently.

Péguy also gives his readers an interesting analysis of the
place of the popular universities within the existing educational
system. In "Vraiment vrai" (Truly True, pp. 398–406) of 1901,
he notes the radical difference between primary and higher
education and the connective role played by secondary education.
The teacher or professor generally has two advantages over
students, his knowledge and his age, while in adult education
he may have only the advantage of knowledge. The problem of
the popular universities is that they must offer "primary education to students who have already received higher education from
life itself" (p. 402). In an effort to solve the problem, attention
should be given to "the press, newspapers, periodicals, and reviews; popular novels; announcements; polemics; the theater;
electoral campaigns; books; politics; posters" (p. 403). Péguy
said that seventy-five years ago. As the editor of the *Cahiers*
Péguy was convinced, as are the professors and parents of every
generation, that "people no longer read" (p. 404), leaving him
and his review in a difficult situation. Péguy's somewhat warped
view of the "good old days" becomes more and more pronounced
as he continues to write. Surprisingly, this essay ends with an
impassioned plea in behalf of Jaurès. Péguy dubs himself "one
of the greatest loyal enemies of Jaurès" (p. 405) and asks everyone to combat Jaurès loyally.

X   *Concerning Reason*

Returning to his concept of the harmonious city in 1901, Péguy
makes an ardent appeal for the good use of reason in "De la

raison" (Concerning Reason, pp. 407–27). His premise is that reason does not proceed from authority, either governmental, military, or religious. The substitution of the Goddess of Reason for the god of any religion is simply a means of replacing one deception with another. In this connection "even the admirable prayer that Renan made on the Acropolis after he had succeeded in understanding perfect beauty no longer makes any sense" (p. 409). Reason does not proceed from parliamentary or demagogic authority nor from the authority of manual or intellectual labor, particularly the government of the intellectuals dreamed of by Renan. In the harmonious city the manual and the intellectual will be combined so that the individual will be freed of economic servitude. Until that time no philosophy of reason, no system of science, art, or philosophy should be attached to Socialism in the name of reason for Socialism itself is "preliminary, preparatory, necessary, indispensable, but insufficient" (p. 414).

Reason does not proceed from parental or Socialist revolutionary authority. Reason does not proceed from journalists with their large followings nor from popularity, terror, force, or suspicion any more than it does from culture, history, or tradition. Above all, reason does not proceed from pedagogy. Péguy seems to have forgotten his own precepts that scientists will have students in the harmonious city, but that artists and philosophers will not when he notes that people more or less agree that "science needs an apprenticeship, but too often deny it in letters, arts, and philosophy" (p. 424). Péguy admits the possible role played by the instincts, the subconscious, vague thoughts, impressions, feelings, sensations, and even passions, but he asks us not to forget that "reason is for humanity the rigorously indispensable condition" (p. 426) and that its means should be applied to the study of social phenomena if we are ever to arrive at the harmonious city.

When a doctor in a small town cancelled his subscription to the *Cahiers* because they were, in comparison with the educational review, *Pages libres (Open Pages)*, useful only to him, Péguy wrote a "Lettre à M. Charles Guieysse" (Letter to Mr. Charles Guieysse, pp. 428–33), the editor of *Pages libres*. As an educator Guieysse was certainly aware of all that Péguy had to say, but Péguy took the opportunity to demonstrate the usefulness of the *Cahiers*. Every student, when he begins the apprenticeship of reality, needs to renew and refresh himself. In order to educate others one needs to educate one's self. Every lesson requires rigorous preparation. Those who live in isolated communities are particularly in need of mental sustenance. "Above all, let us avoid allowing it to be believed that art, philosophy, and science are made only for the bourgeois, and that propaganda alone was made for the Socialists" (p. 432). Educated Socialists must read the works that would bore peasants and workers in order to be able to pass on what they have learned. Such was the role of the *Cahiers* as Péguy conceived it.

XI *Character Assassination*

Péguy had obviously been reproved for his "Personnalités" (Character Sketches or Personal Remarks, pp. 434–84), which were, as we have seen, just short of character assassinations. Jaurès was among those who did not indulge in personal attacks. If Vaillant, Marx's son-in-law Paul Lafargue, and Guesde were responsible for the recently promulgated Socialist constitution that suppressed freedom of thought, justice, and truth, then one should attack such men. In the Dreyfus Affair, for example, "he who was not against the personality of [General Auguste] Mercier [who was among the most guilty in the Affair] was against the personality, then lamentable, of Dreyfus; he who was not against the personality of Vaillant and Guesde was against the personality of Jaurès and thus against the personality of the same Dreyfus" (p. 449). One must take oneself for what he is, ordinary or extraordinary, for as Péguy states, "I abandoned *myself* too much and too long to *others*, and it is above all through myself that I know what can happen to an average ordinary sincere Socialist beaten down for a long time by the strong and deceived for a long time by the cunning" (p. 451). His friends let him down and betrayed him so he arrived at the conclusion that when war has become inevitable, it must be treated as war and not as peace. Only by exercising a moral and personal loyalty can one say what must be said with propriety, probity, and justice in order not to lie.

Thus Péguy will tell the truth as he sees it even if in so doing the *Cahiers* will upset a third of the subscribers, which in fact he hoped they would do. Péguy claimed that he would have much preferred writing stories, novels, dialogues, poems, and dramas to the onerous burden of editing the *Cahiers*. I am not convinced that the truly creative person would allow the one to exclude the other as Péguy himself demonstrated later. Péguy also maintained that there was no real public in France "since the revolutionary lie and the romantic infection" (p. 467). Driven to explain and defend himself for his virulent attacks on others, Péguy took refuge in the cliché "We can only count on ourselves" (twice on p. 469). Any man who says that he has no faith in others and what is worse, has no concept of how to go about having faith in others, makes a strange sort of Socialist indeed. Péguy had thought that work was accomplished by groups, but he learned that they only create agitation. Any work that gets done is realized by one man, again hardly a Socialist concept. The essay is thus among the saddest Péguy published, revealing as it does his despairing lack of faith in others camouflaged by his long-winded defense of his attacks on others in the name of what he called the truth, his own brand of truth.

XII *Elections*

When Péguy wrote in 1902 "Nous devons nous préparer..." (We Must Prepare Ourselves..., pp. 1300–9), he meant for the coming elections because present-day "electoral parliamentarianism is an illness" (p. 1300) best compared to prostitution since it has become the debasement of body, soul, and love. Democracy in America and England produced results no less lamentable than those produced in France and was nothing less than a new type of vice. Must we believe, Péguy asks, "that every acquisition is good and all conservation bad" (p. 1302). To illustrate his point he quotes seven pages from Pascal's thoughts on "'a king without diversion" and on human nature. With Péguy's distaste for democracy and majority rule combined with his lack of faith in others, Pascal's ideas may have seemed extremely apposite to him, but I am not sure Pascal would have appreciated the allusion.

In his lengthy analysis of "Les Elections" (The Elections, pp. 1310–53) of 1902, Péguy, who as far as I know never ran for office in his life, shows a great deal of his own "critical reason after the battle." Placing the blame for Socialist losses after the fact was probably not such a difficult task. French politics remain, for the foreigner, one of the profound mysteries of modern times. Péguy's article would interest the sociologist because he points out the necessity for candidates and parties to analyze population and thus economic and social changes before a campaign begins. He rails against the anticlericals who attack Jaurès because of his daughter's confirmation, but mostly he finds the politicking in the campaign still another symptom of the decomposition of Dreyfusim in France. Nationalism and anti-semitism made progress just at the moment when international politics were assuming a new importance and a new urgency. Péguy can see this but he was so profoundly involved in finger pointing and name calling according to his own concept of the truth that the reader frequently forgets Péguy's larger concern. Politics are, nevertheless, almost always in need of at least one good finger pointer and name caller.

XIII *Misery and Poverty*

When the Société Nouvelle refused to publish a novel, *Jean Coste,* by one of Péguy's teachers, Antonin Lavergne, Péguy published it himself in the *Cahiers.* The book was popular enough to be republished by Ollendorff. This story of a poor village schoolteacher so ground down by poverty that he sees no solution but to kill his family and himself, solicited from Péguy in 1902 his "De Jean Coste" (Concerning Jean Coste, pp. 487–536), a moving essay on misery, a genuine "metaphysics of misery" as one critic put it.[2] Although "misery" in English has somewhat different connotations, I shall stick to Péguy's distinction between *misère* (misery) and *pauvreté* (poverty) (p. 494). The difference in Péguy's mind is not one of degree but of kind. The former might be represented by the hell of the Catholics and the latter by purgatory. In misery there is no hope at all. In poverty there is some glimmer of a possible amelioration of the situation. The problem arises because there are those who are interested in work, the "classics," and those who are only interested in representation, the "romantics." Thus since the institution of parliamentary government those who work are governed by those who represent. As a result the "romantics" have succeeded in creating the myth that there is virtue in misery. The Socialists, however, are clearly aware that economic misery prevents moral and mental improvement because it is an instrument of servitude.

Therefore, the first social duty is to eliminate misery even before the establishment of the harmonious city. Of the three republican virtues, liberty must come first in the form of freedom from economic servitude. The radical difference between fraternity and equality should be noted, however. Fraternity is as old as humanity and the means by which we free our fellowman from misery. Equality was a product of the revolution and can come later in the harmonious city. Péguy returns to his concept of the "revolutionary lie" when he writes that "equality inspired only some particular contestable revolutions: it brought about the English revolution, which willed to the modern world an England neither nationalist, imperialist; it brought about that American revolution, which founded a republic so imperialist, and capitalist; it has not instituted humanity, it has not prepared the city" (pp. 511–12). We can agree, however, with the conclusion to Péguy's sentence: "it only established some democratic governments."

Nevertheless, liberty itself cannot be called liberty if the anticlericals are suppressing the religious orders and persecuting their members. Liberty is either liberty for all or it is not liberty. Without liberty there is no truth. *Jean Coste* exemplified a particular truth of the Third Republic but it was not thereby a political work to be used for political ends. That Péguy in his enthusiasm compared this novel that no one reads today to *Uncle Tom's Cabin, Don Quixote*, and *Robinson Crusoe* need not trouble us. That Péguy wrote a stirring treatise on misery without suggesting means for remedying it need not bother us either, for that was not his goal. What does disturb us is that his message lost itself in all those pages of political incrimination and recrimination.

CHAPTER 3

The Socialist Pamphleteer: 1903–1907

PÉGUY'S essay on "Débats parlementaires" (Parliamentary Debates)[1] proves how little the official stenographic accounts reveal of what actually took place in two sessions of the Chamber of Deputies in 1903. This is only natural, according to Péguy, since all the real business of parliamentary government takes place in the backrooms rather than in open session. Although his motion received seventy-five votes, Jaurès lost in his move to reopen the Dreyfus case. Péguy analyzes the machinations that brought about Jaurès' defeat and in so doing reveals the characters of several deputies as he sees them. Luckily for France and posterity Jaurès' defeat was only temporary.

Already in 1902 Péguy had had intimations that efforts would be made to reopen the case. When Jaurès finally undertook the move, Péguy was infuriated not by what he did but by how he did it, and he said so in "Reprise politique parlementaire" (Parliamentary Political Reprise, pp. 598–661) in 1903. Here, Péguy maintains that the Dreyfus Affair and politics are mutually exclusive. One has to agree, however, with a recent commentator who notes that "much of the responsibility for politicizing Dreyfusism belonged to Péguy himself."[2] Nevertheless, Péguy is right in asserting that left to the military and even the judiciary, the Affair would undoubtedly never have been reopened. Certainly Péguy as the editor of a small journal was in no position to do much except keep the Affair alive in the minds of his readers and that he certainly did. Only a deputy who was necessarily a politician could make the decisive move. Jaurès did that but forgot to alert Péguy personally. I can imagine many reasons why Jaurès might not have taken all the early Dreyfusites, including Péguy, into his confidence in the first stages of his planning. Peguy blamed parliamentary politics for the over-

42

sight. Jaurès was a great orator but he was not a great parliamentary orator, according to Péguy. He could sway crowds but he could not lead a debate in the Chamber, made up as it was of infinite splinter groups. Péguy's analysis of this aspect of French politics is enlightening for the modern reader. Jaurès had to manipulate parliamentary politics in order to be able to operate. What Péguy cannot forgive, however, is that Jaurès had to make his move in a parliamentary, that is in a political lingo that had nothing to do with normal spoken French. Péguy's long description of political language is accurate and amusing, as accurate for American political jargon today as it was for that of the France of 1903. What Péguy cannot really forgive, without ever saying it, is Jaurès' failure in this first attempt. In Jaurès' defense I should say that while Péguy had a clear view of the political scene from without and was adept at discerning ulterior motives after the fact, he never had to operate within the political arena. While Péguy was talking, Jaurès was attempting to act.

I *The Educator*

One of Péguy's essays early in 1904 was his "Avertissement" (Foreword, pp. 1354–88) to the publication of *The New Catechism* by an American of Armenian origin, M. Mangasarian, who was a lecturer of the Independent Religious Society of Chicago. Péguy hesitated to publish the French translation of this rationalist American catechism because all catechisms, religious or lay, are dogmatic and authoritarian and simply substitute one mysticism for another. He decided to publish it as a specimen of what was being done in America, unsure only of how it would be received by the anticlericals in France. The methods and politics of the anticlericals or anticatholics who were the same people as the anti-semites in the early years of the Dreyfus Affair were unacceptable to Péguy. Only Socialism could be effective in replacing Christian morality. Only economic Socialism could prevail. Only popular Socialism could assume the moral authority of religion. Only libertarian Socialism could free the people of the servitudes of the past. One is somewhat surprised to find Péguy, who writes so often of the people and of humanity, maintaining that "the great mass of the populace has a mental and sentimental imbecility" (p. 1366) and for that reason it supported the Voltairian bourgeoisie against the Catholic bourgeoisie. One can be partially conservative and somewhat reactionary, but one must be totally revolutionary. There must be a genius of revolution if it is going to be effected and effective. In contrast, anticatholic anticlerical radicalism is the worst of all politics, conserving and suppressing only according to its own base interests. Revolutionaries would never stoop, of course, to such conniving. Péguy concludes with the dubious observation that because revolution digs more deeply into the inexhausted resources of inner life, "the great men of revolutionary action are eminently great men of great inner life, meditative, contemplative" (p. 1388). I wish Péguy had given us some names.

In "Orléans vu de Montargis" (Orleans Seen from Montargis, pp. 665–75) of 1904, Péguy takes great delight in proving that the "lay and republican ceremonies" of marriage and death are just as ridiculous as the Catholic rituals and even more so because they are imitations of their religious predecessors. Only a Flaubert, to whom the article is dedicated, could have dreamed up such grotesque texts as literal accounts of what took place on these solemn occasions.

II *The Modern World*

Péguy considered "Zangwill" (pp. 679–740) of 1904, purportedly an introduction to Israël Zangwill's novella *Chad Gadya!*, among his most important essays. Actually it is a disquisition on the modern world whose perpetrators were Renan and Taine, the former because he usurped the attributes of an all-knowing God, the latter because he usurped the attributes of God the Creator. The former may have deified man and thus been full of affirmations and presumptions about modern man as the last and best man and the modern world as the last and best. Taine actually believed he could discover the secret of genius by applying modern scientific methods to the domain of history and humanity. The minute the artist, writer, or historian begins to work he chooses, selects. The moment he does so he is no longer free to follow up all the myriad ramifications of Taine's "race, moment, and milieu." He deserts the so-called scientific method with its endless classifications and codifications and creates. Péguy admits it is the old debate between science and art, between the modern historians and those who believe "that there are, for the domain of history and humanity, proper historical and human methods" (p. 739). The scientific method has come a long way since the time of Péguy and shows no signs of stopping. We can only hope that the historical and human methods have made the same progress and will continue to do so.

"Un Essai de monopole" (An Attempt at Monopoly, pp. 741–71) of 1904 served as introduction to "The Primary Education of the Natives in Madagascar" by Raoul Allier. The latter recounts the abuses by the government of Governor-General Joseph Gallieni against the parochial schools in its attempts to establish lay schools and demonstrates its even greater abuses against education in general. Péguy feared that the politics of Jaurès would result in the same kinds of abuses within France as those being perpetrated by French colonialism. That it did not come to pass does not lessen the impact of this account of colonial excesses committed long ago on a faraway island that is still attempting to recover from the injustice.

Early in 1905 Péguy, as historian and editor, was horrified by the necessity of choosing for publication among the daily flood of documents, newspapers, books, and speeches in order to arrive at a semblance of historical truth. I cannot imagine what would have been his reaction to the inundation suffered daily by the individual seventy years later. This increasing flood of "vanities" was "one of the reasons why modern life, in so many respects, is so inferior to so many lives humanity has lived in the course of its history" (p. 773). One situation he knew he could not ignore was the controversy among the members of the French League for the Defense of the Rights of Man and the Citizen. The question was whether the government, under the pretext of protecting the republic, had the right to investigate the private lives and personal opinions of its members, and in order to do so, to encourage denunciation. Some members of the central committee of the League approved, some disapproved and resigned, some disapproved and did not resign in order to try to preserve the original character of the League.

Péguy in "La Délation aux droits de l'homme" (The Denunciation of the Rights of Man, pp. 772–95) sees denunciation as another proof of the decomposition of Dreyfusism in France but this time he includes the decomposition of Socialism, of the parliamentary political regime, and unhappily, perhaps even of the republic itself. Péguy's nationalism reached a new pitch when he declared that France was the only country "in the world that could put all its heart into the elucidation of an individual truth, into the vindication of an individual justice" (p. 782). For him the Dreyfus Affair was "in the history of the world . . . an event as important as the invention and practice of Hellenic harmony, as important as the invention and practice of Christian charity, as important at least as the French revolution" (p. 784). Discounting the hyperbole, I can well imagine Péguy's reaction to the knowledge that governments seventy years later are still snooping into the private lives and opinions not only of their members but of their citizens as well.

III   The Fatherland

"Notre Patrie" (Our Fatherland, pp. 801–53) of 1905 is one of Péguy's great essays in which he displays his talents. He spends ten pages drawing up a list of the perils of internal politics that have threatened the republic in the last five years. Suddenly, the king of Spain pays a visit to Paris and all of Paris, this republican people, "the only people of whom it can be said that it is a people king without making a shameful literary figure of speech" (p. 814) are in the streets to see him. Péguy is happily in their midst watching the king go by when he realizes that these people who will go out to see a king, will not go out to attend the popular universities, which is just as well since Péguy no longer favors them. Victor Hugo is, of course, the poet of the people. Why is it then that his best poems are filled with Napoleon and War? Because he was a "pacifist hypocrite" (p. 835) like the people who asked three incompatible things of the military: parades; exercise of moral reprobation; a subject of inspiration from the past that will assure the present the future spirit of adventure (pp. 832–3). Péguy's literary criticism will be analyzed in a later chapter. The point is that all Paris was shaken by the attempt to assassinate the king of Spain during his visit. Shortly after the king departed unharmed, Paris was shaken again when it learned of the imminent threat of a German invasion. One analyst sees this "sprightly stroll through Paris" as "a secret plea for unity through a common past and heritage."[3] Another calls 1905 "the blow of the gong" during which Péguy passed "from Utopia to the Apocalypse."[4] Indeed 1905 might be looked upon from one point of view as the real beginning of World War I. In any event, Péguy will from now on be looking for its arrival.

The year 1905 was also in many ways the beginning of the Russian revolution. Rather than discuss the tragic events that had taken place in St. Petersburg, Péguy, in his "Courrier de Russie" (Russian Courier, pp. 854–68) writes of a tragic personal event. He describes the happy early days of his friendship with Jaurès when they tramped the woods together reciting Racine and Corneille, Hugo and Vigny, Lamartine and Villon. Years later Jaurès visits Péguy's printer unannounced and misses Péguy. Péguy immediately goes to see the great man only to find him grown old, changed in a way he cannot explain. The two walk the streets of Paris together for a brief time when suddenly Jaurès hails a cab. They shake hands and that is the last time that Péguy sees Jaurès. Jaurès descends into the swamp of politics and the good old days of their early friendship are gone forever. The account of the events in St. Petersburg by Etienne Avenard was first published in part in Jaurès' newspaper *L'Humanité*. In publishing the complete account, Péguy spoke of "France, England, Italy, even America, held under the brutality of the German military menace" (p. 868)—a statement of remarkable foresight for 1905.

IV   *Parallels*

By way of introduction to François Porché's poem "The Supplicants" Péguy published an essay of over sixty-five pages called "Les Suppliants parallèles" (The Parallel Supplicants, pp. 869–935) late in 1905. He opens by drawing a surprising parallel between the tragic supplication of the Russian people to their tsar before the Winter Palace in January 1905 and the supplication of the people of Thebes to OEdipus in Sophocles' *OEdipus the King*. The similarities between the two texts separated by twenty-two centuries are striking. Péguy could not resist giving his readers as well as Leconte de Lisle a long lesson in translating from the Greek into French. His point is that in Greek tragedy the supplicant was not a beggar but a candidate, a representative of the gods, and that the supplicated, the happy, powerful king was destined fatally to become the supplicant. Thus the supplicants of the opening scene become in the end the victors or the liberated, while OEdipus becomes the true supplicant, the blind beggar. Péguy could not know that in twelve years the tsar and his supplicants would also reverse roles. One French Socialist wanted to dash off to Poland to aid the oppressed Poles. The Socialist party also organized a meeting to aid the Russian revolutionary movement at which Péguy's old friends-enemies would be speaking including Jaurès, Edouard Vaillant, one of the founders of the French Socialist party Jean Allemane, one of the founders of the League of Rights Francis de Pressensé, and Paul Lafargue. Péguy could not restrain his disdain for such ineffectual parliamentary politics. He counted the efforts as a waste of time since "all the liberty of the world will be risked on the banks of the Meuse River and in the valleys of the Argonne" (p. 921). This too was an acute perception for 1905. Péguy spent the last few pages lamenting the loss of the study of Greek in the curriculum of the new state-regulated schools and the low esteem in which the study of the humanities was held.

"Louis de Gonzague" (pp. 936–49) of late 1905 is Péguy's new year's wish to his subscribers. Péguy states that we learned from the Jews that "the temporal salvation of humanity has an infinite price" (p. 938) and from Christians like Pascal that "eternal salvation has an infinitely infinite price" (p. 939). As Platonists we know our republic and as Kantians we know our moral obligations. We must continue to demonstrate a courage that is a "French courage." To illustrate his point Péguy tells the story of St. Louis de Gonzague who is interrupted while playing ball and is asked what he would do if he learned that the final judgment would take place in twenty-five minutes. He replies that he would continue to play ball. The saint's response is identical to Péguy's. Thus, Péguy will continue to publish the *Cahiers* in the face of the German menace. While Péguy has always tried to do his most and his best, he has never deceived himself except in placing much too much confidence in men who do not deserve it. He concludes with "it does not depend upon us that the event be set in motion. But it does depend upon us to do our duty" (p. 949).

A short story by Jérôme and Jean Tharaud did not fill one of the *Cahiers* of 1906 so Péguy wrote at length in "Cahiers de la Quinzaine" (pp. 950–87) about the direction, management, and administration of his review. In addition to publishing the Tharauds and Romain Rolland, Péguy was in close communication with Paul Desjardins of the Union for the Truth. He also had some contact with several eminent men, some of whom were mentioned in the first chapter. Péguy would have liked to publish the "political, economic and social history" (p. 957) of the *Cahiers* but political events had not left him the time. In reference to the economic problems of the review, he made a wonderful observation that "Not to pay like everyone else, [is] the dream of all our Frenchmen" (p. 960). Péguy also explained and perhaps even tried to excuse his own prickly personality by maintaining that "a good administrator is a man who knows no friends at all" (p. 963). One hopes he was being ironical in devoting so much time to determining what was precisely personal and impersonal, public and private, and so forth before deciding to publish it. He ended on the sad note that in situations such as that of being a governmental informer he had to break friendships of twenty years in order to print the truth.

V   *Genius and Talent*

Péguy proved that he was not a philosopher or even an historian in "De la Situation faite à l'histoire et à la sociologie dans les temps modernes" (Concerning the Status of History and Sociology in Modern Times, pp. 991–1030) of 1906. His analysis of the relationships between history and sociology is debatable but it permitted him to defer discussing sociology until the end of his essay. According to his view primary teachers are too preoccupied with the maintenance of discipline to have time for the hesitations of history. University professors are so busy with their hesitations, their quibbling about details, that they have no time to affirm anything. Thus the best teachers of history are found in the secondary schools, for while they are less preoccupied with discipline they are also learning the realities of life as a sound and practical basis for their teaching. Péguy's view of secondary teaching appears somewhat idealized.

Péguy also states that the great error of modern times has been to believe that instruments and methods are everything while probity counts for nothing. Whereupon he returns to his favorite themes. Genius is not simply a higher degree of talent but is of a completely different order. Michelet is the example of the historical genius, while "All the intelligent people we know ... have a mortal hatred for genius and the works of genius" (p. 1009). Péguy then takes up his favorite whipping-boy, Renan, and expatiates again on how he is the cause of the modern predicament. A whole generation of men between the ages of thirty-seven and forty-eight in 1906 accepted Renan's *The Future of Science* as a bible and thus made a religion of historical science. I do, however, rather like Péguy's characterization of Fénelon as the Renan of the seventeenth century, although I am convinced he gave much too much credit, and blame to Renan. If one is going to tell the truth he must be prepared to lose friends. The great example is the Dreyfus Affair which Péguy is now convinced has entered the domain of history. Under the influence of Renan, the modern world has simply substituted one dogma for another resulting in part in "this great intellectual indigence of modern times" (p. 1026). In view of the works of Freud, Planck, and Einstein, to name only a few, the period was hardly an intellectual desert.

VI *Anticlericalism Again*

Late in 1906 Péguy published "De la Situation faite au parti intellectuel dans le monde moderne" (Concerning the Status of the Intellectual Party in the Modern World, pp. 1031–78), in which he traces the anticlericalism of the government back to Renan. When Renan left the church, the church handled him very gingerly. So gingerly, according to Péguy, that its liberal attitude was more modern than Christian, thus explaining the present weakness of the church. But Renan also retained so much of his religious training and thought in what he wrote later that Péguy maintains that neither a non-Catholic, a non-former Catholic, a non-Christian, nor a non-Jew could understand what Renan is really saying. Péguy asserts that there are two kinds of friends, those who want to dominate their friends and those who are happy simply in the happiness of their friends. There are also two kinds of men, those who want to have followers and those who do not. In both cases, Renan is obviously the first type. That he intended to be a domineering friend should be kept in mind by the reader of *The Future of Science.* That he wanted followers is proved by the inauguration of the monument in his honor in his hometown Tréguier. The reader might be happier with Péguy's distinctions if he did not have the uncomfortable feeling that Péguy automatically classified himself as the opposite of Renan both as friend and man. Péguy goes on to point out the connection between intellectual ambition and political ambition, a debatable idea at best. Nevertheless, the many intellectuals in government had promised a philosophically, religiously, and metaphysically neutral government. Instead, René Viviani, the Minister of Labor, praised publicly the anticlericalism of the government. Anticlericalism or atheism is a metaphysics as surely as Christianity or any other form of religion. The state is a manufacturer of matches and laws, and has now gone into the business of manufacturing metaphysics which is none of its business. Péguy's attack against anticlericalism was an admirable one in the name of freedom for all. Poor old Renan certainly took a beating in the process, however.

VII *Literary Style*

Much has been written about Péguy's extraordinarily long sentences; some critics defend them as the microcosm of his long essays, others dismiss them as unintelligible aberrations.

An analysis of the concluding seventeen-line sentence of the
second paragraph of the preceding essay will serve as an example of what Péguy could achieve. Here, Péguy discusses man's
relationship to the church:

Ainsi elle [l'Eglise] est liée à eux [ceux qui l'ont quitée décemment],
elle demeure attachée à eux par une sorte d'entente secrète, une
qualité particulière, unique, rare, d'ancienne intelligence conservée,
aromateuse, essentielle, un peu capiteuse, une connivence, d'encens,
de sacristie, de tabernacle, d'armoire et ensemble d'autel, de linge
blanc frais pur et de pauvre vieille dentelle jaunie, de vieille armoire
de grande famille, un commun souvenir qui va de la commodité
mobilière et usagère du sacristain jusqu'à la divine autorité du prêtre.
une collusion, une entente particulière par-dessus la tête du public,
du vulgaire, des tiers, particulièrement par-dessus la tête de ceux
qui sont les plus vulgaires de tous ces tiers, et qui certainement n'y
comprennent plus rien du tout, par-dessus la tête de ceux qui se sont
faits hautement les partisans, les protecteurs, les intronisateurs improvisés du déporté dans sa nouvelle religion. (pp. 1031–2)

Thus she [the Church] is tied to them [those who have left the
church in a proper way], she remains attached to them by a sort of
secret agreement, a particular quality, unique, rare, of former intelligence preserved, aromatic, essential, a bit sensuous, a connivance
of incense, of sacristy, of tabernacle, of clothes-closet and the whole
of the altar, of linen, white, fresh, pure, and of poor old yellowed
lace, of the old clothes-closet of a great family, a common memory
which goes from the mobile and useful convenience of the sacristan
to the divine authority of the priest, a collusion, a particular agreement over the head of the public, of the vulgar, of the third persons,
particularly over the head of those who are the most vulgar of all
these third persons, and who certainly no longer understand anything at all, over the head of those who have loftily made themselves
the partisans, the protectors, the impromptu enthroners of the
deportee in his new religion.

Like most good concluding sentences this one begins with
"Thus" (*Ainsi*). Then for emphasis Péguy reiterates "she is tied
to them, she remains attached to them" (*elle est liée à eux, elle
demeure attachée à eux*), thus insisting upon the nuance of
difference between "tied" and "attached" with the important word

the verb "remains." She is tied to those who like Renan have left her by a double triad of means beginning with "a sort of secret agreement" (*par une sorte d'entente secrète*) followed by the immediate contrast of "a particular quality" (*une qualité particulière*) and continued by "a connivance" (*une connivence*) based on "a common memory" (*un commun souvenir*) that becomes "a collusion" (*une collusion*) that is "a particular agreement" (*une entente particulière*). This movement from "a sort of secret agreement" to "a particular agreement" is emphasized by the triple use of "particular," twice as an adjective (*particulière*) and once as an adverb (*particulièrement*).

Triadic structures dominate the paragraph from "a quality" (*une qualité*) that is "particular, unique, rare" (*particulière, unique, rare*) to a "former intelligence" (*ancienne intelligence*) or understanding that is "preserved, aromatic, essential" (*conservée, aromateuse, essentielle,* with *aromateuse* an elegant neologism for *aromatique*), and also "somewhat sensuous" (*un peu capiteuse,* which thus rhymes with *aromateuse*). It is also "a *connivance*" (*une connivence*), a much stronger term with overtones of pretended ignorance and secret cooperation, "of incense, of sacristy, of tabernacle, of clothes-closet, of altar, of linen" (*d'encens, de sacristie, de tabernacle, d'armoire et ensemble d'autel, de linge*), a double triad. The linen (*de linge*) is "white, fresh, pure" (*blanc frais pur*) and is contrasted with "the lace" (*dentelle*) that is "poor, old . . . yellowed" (*pauvre vieille . . . jaunie*). Both the words "clothes-closet" (*armoire*) and "old" (*vieille*) are repeated by the "old clothes-closet of a great family" (*de vieille armoire de grande famille*), turning the closet for the vestments into a closet for the whole great family of the church with overtones of luxury and close relationships. Both the church and the apostate share "a common souvenir" (*un commun souvenir*) which contrasts with the "great family" that immediately precedes it. The memory includes "the convenience" (*la commodité*) of the poor sacristan (*du sacristain*) who is a movable convenience like a useful piece of furtniture (*mobilière et usagère*). *Sacristain* echoes *sacristie* used earlier while *usagère* is another of Péguy's neologisms which give him the opportunity to insist on the ending *-ère* found in *particulière, mobilière, vulgaire,* and *tiers.* Con-

trasting with this common convenience is "the divine authority of
the priest" (*la divine autorité du prêtre*), with "divine" taking
on ironic overtones. The connivance and the memory become
"a collusion" (*une collusion*) with its insistence on active and
knowing cooperation, "a particular understanding" (*une entente
particulière*), by means of which they have gone "over the head"
(*par-dessus la tête*) of three groups, "the public, the vulgar, the
third persons" (*du public, du vulgaire, des tiers*). *Tiers* can
mean the third persons who are not party to or privy to what is
going on, but it also suggests the "third estate" (*tiers état*), all
those who were neither of the nobility or of the clergy under
the ancient regime. *Une entente particulière par-dessus la tête*
becomes *particulièrement par-dessus la tête* in this repetition in
which *vulgaire* becomes "the most vulgar" (*les plus vulgaires*)
while *des tiers* becomes "of all these third persons" (*de tous ces
tiers*). These third persons are undoubtedly the lay members
of the church who haven't the slightest idea of all the scheming
and conniving that is going on behind the scenes (*qui certainement n'y comprennent plus rien du tout*). The third use of
"over the head" includes even "those who have loftily made
themselves" (*ceux qui se sont faits hautement*) three things,
"the partisans, the protectors, the impromptu enthroners" (*les
partisans, les protecteurs, les intronisateurs improvisés*). The
irony is that this "deportee" (*déporté*) is going to be "enthroned"
"in his new religion" (*dans sa nouvelle religion*), whatever it
may be, and under the scheming auspices of the very religion
that made of him a "deportee."

With this last expression Péguy has gone from the general to
the specific in this sentence, from the undifferentiated plural
object pronoun "them" (*eux*) at the beginning of the sentence to
the specific singular noun *déporté* at the end. What was linked
and attached has now become separated but with so many
strings still tying it to the church that it is almost as if no
separation had taken place. Thus Péguy could maintain that
Renan was so impregnated with the ideas and religious style
of the church that all he wrote could only be understood by those
with a Catholic or Jewish background. Péguy always defended
the freedom of the church against the anticlericals but this
picture of religious politics does not augur well for his welcome

into the church after his return to Catholicism in 1908. Nor unfortunately will this close analysis hold true for all of his long sentences. The reader frequently gets lost only shortly after Péguy in endless meanderings.

VIII *The Modern World Again*

By way of answer to a letter provoked by the previous essay, Péguy published "De la Situation faite à l'histoire et à la sociologie et de la situation faite au parti intellectuel dans le monde moderne" (Concerning the Status of History and Sociology and Concerning the Status of the Intellectual Party in the Modern World, pp. 1079–1111) early in 1907. In it he states that the great error of modern intellectual metaphysics lies in believing that the total reality of man and of creation can be known through the manipulation of filing cards correctly arranged. Through the abuse of history and the use of sociology the modern intellectual does not see that modern theories are only the transposition into modern language of ancient theories. Modern man has not developed better theories, only better techniques, and has thus confused the real linear progress of techniques with the imaginary linear progress of theories. Metaphysics is the only search for knowledge that is direct, whereas physics can only be an attempt at the indirect search for knowledge through the intermediary of the senses. We may have surpassed the first locomotives but no man can say that he has surpassed Plato. We do not surpass philosophies which are nothing less than the languages of creation; they simply no longer speak to us. At that moment we begin to feel ourselves liberated and it is truly and only in that sense that modern man is free. The modern world was obviously not to Péguy's taste.

As his titles grew longer and longer, his essays got windier and windier. The case in point is "De la Situation faite au parti intellectuel dans le monde moderne devant les accidents de la gloire temporelle" (Concerning the Status of the Intellectual Party in the Modern World in the Face of Accidents of Temporal Glory, pp. 1115–1214) of 1907. The subject, simply stated, is his old favorite, Taine and Renan and this dreadful modern world. In such a world "the base (*turpides*) souls go to turpi-

tude; the servile souls go to servitude. The imbeciles go to
honesty" (p. 1117). Péguy himself, as a simple corrector of
copy and printer's proofs, was obviously among the latter. As
an avowed non-Catholic Péguy could still hold that death for
him was the end of life rather than the beginning of eternity,
but his attitude would change in less than a year. Primarily
he was unhappy about professors like Gustave Lanson in state
universities who were exerting unlimited power. That Péguy
"certainly exaggerated the direct political power wielded by
what he came to describe as the 'intellectual party'"[5] is undoubtedly true. According to him the glory of olden times that
was a spiritual power has become in the modern world an intellectual, temporal power. He characterizes himself as "a poor
innocent, a poor man who has, unlike the great contemporary
geniuses, no infinite resources" (p. 1125). Péguy may not have
had the money but he certainly had the requisite false modesty.

Péguy's idea that in the modern world the barricades have
been replaced by the cashier's window is appealing. For Péguy,
money is obviously the key to modern life. But then, hasn't it
always been the key to life in one form or another? Even more
questionable is his contention that "Under the ancient regimes,
glory was an almost uniquely spiritual power" (p. 1137). Just
how ancient the regime would have to be in order for this statement to be true is unclear, since a regime just because it was
old was not therefore necessarily more spiritual. Péguy again
mourned the passing of the study of Greek and Greek civilization
as well as Christianity in the state controlled schools. One can
almost forgive Péguy his verbosity after reading his magnificent
panegyric to the city of Paris, to France and the Beauce, and
to the Loire. Today's itinerant youth would be pleased with
Péguy's praise of the back pack but I am not sure that all the
foot-sloggers of the revolution and the empire were so convinced
of what they were doing or why they were doing it. When Péguy
begins to exalt heroism, his militarism begins to show through.
Just as he berated the anticlericals, so he berated the antimilitar-
ists. For anyone who could read it should have been perfectly
clear that Péguy could hardly wait to be a hero and, more
specifically, a military hero. Of course, the truly great hero is
the dead hero.

Péguy did not realize, as Proust puts it, that "If another war were to come, patriotism would take another form, and one would not even be interested to know whether the chauvinistic author had been a Dreyfusite or not."[6] The use of Péguy by certain Vichy elements in World War II more than proves Proust's point. In spite of the vast energy and numerous pages Péguy expanded on the Dreyfus Affair, the reader learns almost more about it from Proust's novel than from Péguy's heated essays, even though names like Galliffet and Reinach mean no more to the reader of fiction than to the reader of expository prose. In like manner the reader learns almost more about some of the weaknesses of the "Sorbonnards" from Proust's lone character Brichot than from all the denunciations of them by Péguy.

CHAPTER 4

The Catholic Pamphleteer: 1909–1910

OBVIOUSLY neither Péguy's style nor his subject matter changed radically after his return to Catholicism in 1908. Almost everything Péguy, the avowed Socialist, wrote up to that time revealed a deep religious sentiment. Everything he wrote after that date was still filled with Socialist fervor. Socialism and Catholicism were by no means mutually exclusive in Péguy's mind. I have used the titles "The Socialist Pamphleteer" and "The Catholic Pamphleteer" for convenience only in order to distinguish the two periods of his life. The fact is, Péguy published nothing in the *Cahiers* between October 1907 and June 1909. The first essay Péguy published after this hiatus treats many of the same subjects in much the same way as before. The reader begins to wonder if Péguy will ever find something new to say. What he had to say that was different, he expressed in the many poetic works he was writing in the same period.

I *The Vanquished*

The first essay of 1909 was "A nos amis, à nos abonnés" (To Our Friends, To Our Subscribers).[1] After a desperate plea for financial assistance from the friends of and the subscribers to the *Cahiers*, Péguy recounts the fifteen years of his heroic, epic struggle to make a success of the review with no money. He forgets to mention that he had had money, the forty thousand francs of his wife's dowry, much of which he lost in his first publishing venture. In his idealism, he again refuses to accept advertising or to attempt publicity. This may be the way to operate a review in the harmonious city. It was hardly the way to succeed in early twentieth-century Paris.

The *Cahiers* were and are, nevertheless, a magnificent monument to his success, the "national archives of those seething

58

years of the new century"[2] as one observer puts it. Péguy felt
he had achieved what he did in spite of "this time of universal
sabotage," "this so barbarous time" (p. 5), in spite of the flood
of pornography that was inundating Paris and the political corruption that was eroding the soul of France. He had achieved
all this without a preconceived or narrowly defined program, a
literary "chapel," or cliques. He felt he had created a society,
a family of kindred spirits, a friendship, a city, partly from
what he had learned from men like his late friends, the Jewish
journalist Bernard-Lazare who died in 1903 and the dramatist
Eddy Marix who died in 1908.

Péguy's greatest crusade was the Dreyfus Affair and the subsequent decomposition of Dreyfusism in France which he felt
still dominated everyone's life, for his was a sacrificed generation. Péguy could not know how prophetic his words would
become as a result of World War I. He was convinced the men
of his generation were as good as the men of the Commune, the
Revolution, and the Empire. His description of war is moving
yet somehow suspect. Péguy was too interested in war and in
death and dying. He quotes at length the death scene of Napoleon's Marshal Lannes who died of wounds in the hospital and
compared it with the death of Alphonse Baudin on the barricades in the revolution of 1851. The names Baudouin, Baudin,
and Boudon haunt Péguy's life. Ostensibly Clio, the muse of
history and, as Péguy calls her, the daughter of memory, is
speaking. Actually it is Péguy who claims "I am not interested
in people who take fifty years to die in bed" (p. 20). It is Péguy
who says "What I need is a death with a date" (p. 27).

But Clio can only speak through the echoes of reality, not
through reality itself. Péguy states unequivocally, "We are the
vanquished" (p. 36), the vanquished sons of the vanquished
France of the Franco-Prussian War. Almost forty years after the
event Péguy was still bearing the guilt for a defeat he was born
too late to witness. He then expresses the debatable idea that
there is some impurity in every success or victory or good fortune, while there can only be true and total purity in misfortune. Péguy will express somewhat the same idea in *Eve* when
he calls "poverty, pain, and privation" "supernatural goods."
Péguy would seem to have fallen victim of the very myth he

denounced in "De Jean Coste" of 1902, that there is somehow a
virtue in misery. His profound conviction is that only one
hundred twenty years after the revolution, its work has been
undone, reduced to nothing. In his enthusiasm he maintains
that "military force is not only a brutal force, but above all a sort
of pure force, I mean a force more purely force" (p. 39). This
statement is certainly true but Péguy goes on to assert, "Defending an order, or a new disorder, [our pacifists and our anti-
militarists] will make moreover some marvelous wars" (p. 41).
Certainly, the wars they have made are not any more marvelous
than those made by the undeclared but would-be militarists
like Péguy.

What seems to be Péguy's problem in this essay? He speaks
with an eighteen year-old about the Dreyfus Affair only to
learn to his horror that what he knows as reality the boy only
know historically. This reaction is a perfectly normal trauma
for every thirty-five year-old. It's called growing older. For this
reason Clio, the muse of history, can only speak through echoes,
the memory of events, rather than through reality itself. Péguy
draws the rather hasty conclusion that one can thus only be
friends with those of the same time and age, the same company,
schooling, society, world, and of the same class. He does have
the good sense and the clear eye to conclude that all who were
so involved in the Dreyfus Affair will only be old fools (*vieilles
bêtes*, p. 50) for those who come after, and those who come
after will soon be everyone.

A variant of part of the preceding essay was found and published posthumously under the title "Nous sommes des vaincus"
(We Are the Vanquished, pp. 55–92), taken from the opening
sentence. Péguy's reasons for not publishing the text are obvious.
He begins by again drawing up a list of all the demagogies
plaguing France, culminating with the demagogy of state exer-
cised by Emile Combes, the anticlerical prime minister, which
explains the title. Péguy's aim is to state what he wants to ac-
complish with the *Cahiers* and to try to see what they are going
to become in the face of such difficulties. If Péguy cannot say
he has exhausted all his bitterness in administering the review,
he can say he has exhausted all ingratitude. Patently, Péguy
could not tax his friends, subscribers, and collaborators with

ingratitude. He wanted every author published in the *Cahiers* to subscribe to them. Péguy, better than anyone else, should have realized that if every writer subscribed to every review in which he was published, he would soon be bankrupt. Having broken with the League for the Rights of Man on the issue of the government's right to spy on its own members, Péguy could not forgive the League's *Bulletin* its one hundred thousand franc yearly budget, particularly in view of the little it accomplished.

The subscribers to the *Cahiers*, the collective boss, treated poor Péguy with a harshness that would be found in few industries. He also admits that he has ruined his wife and children and goes on to describe the unpleasant aspects of being an editor, one of which is the refusals he must make. He writes at length of the young would-be writer from the provinces recommended to him by Anatole France. The recommendation cost France nothing and assured his continued popularity. The recommendation cost Péguy an unpleasant scene and in the end a subscriber. Since money dominates everything, it is necessary to sell oneself in order to make a lot of money. The only writer Péguy knows who sold himself only a little was Romain Rolland, one of the few profitable authors published by the *Cahiers*. Péguy did well not to publish this article with its somewhat indiscriminate praise and blame. He did, however, foretell one of his most important essays to come, "L'Argent" (Money).

II *The Pagan Soul*

A second posthumous manuscript has been called "Clio, dialogue de l'histoire et de l'âme païenne" (Clio, A Dialogue of History and the Pagan Soul, pp. 95–308), a part of which dates from 1909, the other part from 1912. It begins as a precious conceit, ponderously precious as only Péguy could make it. Clio, the eldest of the nine muses, is a poor old woman with so much past and without any future. To exhaust the question of the past, to exhaust the reality of pagan antiquity is, of course, impossible. Nevertheless, one knows nothing except through history. Ancient wisdom was the product of one race, divided between the Apollonian and the Dionysian. All the muses were naturally Apollonian and certainly Péguy was also. He was

Dionysian only in the length of his essays, in the frenzy of his attacks on others, and in his death.

The greatest source of our knowledge of early Greece is Homer. When Péguy says "reading is the common act, the common operation of the reading and the read" (*du lisant et du lu*, p. 105), one can almost hear today's structuralists speaking. Reading is "the real completion of the work," "a high, supreme and singular, a disconcerting responsibility" (p. 106). Thus every work is "perpetually completed as incomplete" (p. 107). The author presents us with a work and we bring to it memory, but memory and history form a right angle. If history is parallel to the event, then memory is central and axial with it. They meet but they are not the same thing. As a result, "perhaps the most delicate problem of esthetics . . . is essentially a problem of history, a problem of the very organization of memory" (p. 124). Taking as an example Monet's twenty-seven or thirty-five different views of the "Water Lilies," Péguy maintains that geniuses have perhaps never done anything but begin again their admirable "Water Lilies." In answering the question of which is the best painting, the first or the last, Péguy would say the first. The logical theory of progress according to which the modern world operates would dictate the last as the best because of the experience gained. But this theory is inorganic and ignores the laws of Bergsonian duration.

As an example of genius Péguy chooses Victor Hugo. He analyzes how Hugo and Beaumarchais could both take the folksong "Malbroug s'en va-t-en guerre" (Marlborough Goes Off to War) the one making of it a *danse macabre*, the other a romance. After discussing Beaumarchais' third and almost unknown play *L'Autre Tartufe, ou la Mère coupable* (*The Other Tartufe or the Guilty Mother*) of 1792, Péguy returned to Hugo several times, to Homer, and concludes with Hugo. His literary criticism will be discussed later. While making many acute obervations Péguy does not forget his old enemies Ernest Lavisse, Combes, Camille Pelletan, Combes' minister of the marine, and of course Jaurès. The sociologist Emile Durkheim gets his come-uppance as well as the historians Charles-Victor Langlois (of whom we shall hear much more), Charles Seignobos, and Gustave Bloch, and the literary historian Gustave Lanson.

In defining a masterpiece Péguy maintains that it is the tone and content that make a work, infinitely more than its significance. He also writes that an author, if he is truly an author, lives in a perpetual brush (*affleurement*, p. 197) of texts, ideas, and worlds. This constant bumping against one another of texts reminds one of the contemporary experimental author Michel Butor in the composition of his *Illustrations* where he places parts of one of his poems within parts of another, thus creating new possibilities of meaning. Calling on posterity where a work is concerned is, however, "an illusion of perspective" (p. 218) since it is a call for a continued but final judgment that will never come. The work is truly "completed as incomplete."

Most interesting, however, is what Péguy reveals about himself in this essay. One admirable trait that remained constant was his refusal to give in to any temporal tyranny, either radical or clerical. Since the Sorbonne, the École Normale, and the political parties had robbed him of his youth, he has become one of God's faithful sinners of the common species. For this reason he regrets that the modern world has all but banished Christianity. Such proscription limits liberty. He asserts that "since man has existed, no man has ever been happy" (p. 229). Albert Camus' Caligula said "Men die and they are not happy." Péguy scorns all those who thought the Dreyfus Affair would end with a judgment by the Court of Appeals. Given the degeneration of the spirit of Dreyfusism in the modern world, the Affair was indeed a dead issue. When Clio says that it would take her a day to write the history of a second, a year for a minute, a life for an hour, an eternity for a day, one thinks of Butor's ill-fated hero's attempts to do just that in his novel *Degrés*. The problem is that in order to write ancient history the references are lacking. For the writing of modern history, there are too many references.

Taking Homer as a source, Péguy vaunts antique purity. Unfortunately, Péguy's attitude is most likely another example of his own "illusion of perspective." Antiquity was not all that pure, except perhaps as Homer portrays it. In Homer, the greatness of antiquity lies in its heroes. Clio, sensitive to this fact, claims that she lacks the greatest and the most beautiful thing in Homer, an early death, and above all an early death in military combat. Clio may be speaking, but Péguy is doing the identifying.

Péguy saw man as a poet at twenty, a memorialist and chronicler at forty, and as an historian at fifty. A "man will always prefer to measure himself, rather than see himself" (pp. 286–7). Péguy could measure himself at forty as a memorialist and a chronicler, which in many respects he was, but he could not see himself as a mere historian at fifty. Péguy's problem was that his forty years were almost exactly the years of the Third Republic which knew no wars between the Franco-Prussian War of 1870–71 and the war of 1914–18. To be a hero, a military hero, a military hero who died before he was fifty was obviously already Péguy's desire. The essay concludes with Clio's remarks to him: "You do not imagine yourself presiding at the fiftieth series of your *Cahiers*. But you can imagine very well, and I can imagine with you (my child, she said to me with great tenderness), what you will think the day of your death" (p. 308). Péguy had two years to live. This one hundred eighty-nine page essay combines some interesting ideas that were much more "modern" than Péguy would have admitted with some unusual observations and intellectual nonsense.

III *The Carnal Soul*

"Véronique, dialogue de l'historie et de l'âme charnelle" (Veronica, A Dialogue of History and the Carnal Soul, pp. 311–500) of 1909 was also published posthumously. Although it has been given the title "Veronica," Clio is still talking about Monet and his "Water Lilies" that have now become twenty-five and thirty-seven in number. She again chooses Hugo as an example of genius because he sees the world as if it has just been created. In fact, he sees what Homer, Hesiod, Pindar, and Aeschylus did not see. Obviously, their place in time has caused them to see different physical worlds, but the larger question is what they intuited in the act of observing. If history creates genius since genius can only be recognized in retrospect, then the secret of genius is its eternal youth and its lack of memory. Péguy, unable to resist military metaphors, compared the memory of ordinary men to military impedimenta while genius speaks like a child unencumbered with a past.

The central question is, then, one of age. Péguy's morbid preoccupation with age permeates the whole essay. Taking cities and their age as an example, he notes that the founding of a city is a sacred act. Aside from the cities purposely created by Alexander, Hadrian, Peter the Great, and others, one doubts that the natural agglomerations of people along waterways and near ports were always aware of the sacredness of their act. The founding of a family is an equally significant act while the supreme act was the founding of the city of God by Jesus, a city that was at the same time spiritual and carnal. One can understand why Péguy, who had just announced his return to Catholicism, did not publish this essay. His attack on the clerics and curés would put him solidly in the camp of the anticlericals. According to him they have a mistaken idea of creation, an erroneous conception of the operation of grace. They are convinced that God works for them, forgetting that it is their job to work for Him. They have forgotten that the city of God is both spiritual and carnal, eternal and temporal, thus helping to bring about the deChristianization of the modern world through a fault of mystique. Their avarice and lack of belief in anything stems from a lack of knowledge of the self. They have forgotten the temporal, and that Jesus was a temporal man in a temporal world. To deny the eternal is also one of the great temptations of the century. The only agreeable thing Péguy can find to say about the curés is that they are just as odious now as they were thirty years ago when he left them. Such opinions would hardly assure Péguy a warm welcome into the church.

But Péguy reserves his harshest criticism, as usual, for the modern world. The religion of progress is the greatest modern heresy from which his generation, the first of the moderns, is suffering. People like Combes and Léon Blum are the politicians of deChristianization but the church is also at fault. Hugo, exiled like a sinner, is excommunicated. However, he is still French just as the excommunicated is still a Christian. The Catholics have confused the deChristianization of the modern world with the problem of the excommunicated sinner. Péguy indulges in a long homily on the gospel according to St. Matthew in order to demonstrate that Jesus was a carnal soul like mortal man. As man he was temporal, as a god he was eternal.

The cleric's confusion and even refusal to reconcile the two has ended in "the triumphant scandal of the modern world" (p. 491). The truth is, paganism and Christianity were both founded on misfortune. The only difference is that paganism created misfortune while Christianity created the misery of the temporal and the sinful.

Péguy also did not publish the manuscript because he was unable to complete it. He seldom corrected his writings, except to make additions. Nevertheless, the "modern" reader finds it difficult to forgive him for writing a paragraph eighty-four pages long even though whole books of one paragraph and indeed of one sentence have been at times a twentieth-century fad. The only "modern" idea Péguy expresses is his comparison of the founding of a city to the birth of a child, to the workings of genius. These acts are the taking up of a temporal veil, a certain date before which there was nothing, after which there is history, a departure towards the future, a process that has been put in motion and will end no one knows where. In going from nothing to something, to something new, every man, says Clio, will experience "the taste of me, the secret taste, the after-taste of me," producing an anxiety "that has its own taste, an ipseity that no man worthy of the name of man will ever confuse with any other" (pp. 344–5). Thus man becomes historical man and is filled with anxiety. Péguy almost sounds like the existentialist Sartre speaking. Otherwise the essay is a long religious divagation of dubious orthodoxy and of doubtful interest to anyone but the Péguy enthusiast.

IV *Our Youth*

"Notre Jeunesse" (Our Youth, pp. 504–655) of July 1910 is one of Péguy's four or five best known essays. He wrote it as a reply to an essay, "Apology for Our Past" by his friend Daniel Halévy, that appeared in the *Cahiers* in April. Péguy begins by introducing the papers of a family of Fourierist republicans, the Milliets, being published in the present issue. He turns very soon, however, to his point of difference with Halévy which is that while he agrees that a number of the faithful have maintained the republican tradition and mystique, he also believes that his generation and that of Halévy are the last representatives of attempts at such a conservation. After them another age, a completely different world of those who no longer believe in anything and are proud of it, will begin. In short, derepublicanization and deChristianization in the modern world have led to a "demistification" resulting in modern sterility.

The generation of Péguy and Halévy was caught between two generations. Péguy's only hope is that the generation of their grandchildren will again be a mystical generation. In the meantime, his generation will be denigrated by the generation that went before as well as by the one that came immediately after. "That is," as Péguy puts it, "the common fate of anyone who tries to tell a little truth" (p. 510). It is also, I might add, the fate of anyone who tries to pass off his truth as the only truth. According to Péguy, in the modern world thoughts have become ideas, an instinct has become a proposition, the organic has become logic, the republic had become a thesis and has thus become prostrate. The monarchies that surrounded the Third Republic were in the same situation, for the mystique of monarchy had been forgotten like that of the republic. Péguy then asks his much quoted question, "The degradation of the mystique into politics, is it not a common law" (p. 517) and repeats it in its better known form, "All begins in mystique and ends in politics" (p. 518). According to such a law the Christian mystique has ended in clerical politics. When Péguy saw what the clerics had made of the saints, he was not surprised to see what the parliamentarians had made of his heroes. Péguy's belief that a mystique ends inevitably in politics is convincing because a mystique that remains only a mystique is nothing but a theory, a hypothesis, an abstraction, unused and useless. Only when the mystique is transformed into practice does it acquire meaning. Péguy was great at theorizing. He was less successful at implementing his theories.

According to Péguy, 1881 was the important year when the intellectual party began to dominate the political scene. Any man who, in order to remain faithful to a mystique, refuses to participate in political games, is called a traitor. If a mystique can only be realized by politics, then it is unclear what alternatives Péguy had. His point was, of course, that the mystique of the Dreyfus Affair had degenerated into politics, and there he was right. Politics proved in the end the only means of concluding the Affair. That it eventually did so more or less honorably after a long period of disgraceful maneuvering, was the belated proof of the power of the mystique—and of politics.

Péguy was not so unhappy with politicians in general as he was with those who left the teaching profession to become politicians. Such men were generally not from primary education where culture was taught, nor from secondary education which was still the citadel of culture, but from higher education, a point Péguy had made in a slightly different way in "The Status of History and Sociology." Péguy's prime example was still Jaurès, a politician with a doctorate whom Péguy did not hesitate to call a cad and a coward (*un pleutre*, p. 539). Péguy would like to write his own confessions which would be those of a man faithful to the mystique of the Dreyfus Affair. He and his friends were "infinitely full, infinitely swollen with military virtues" (p. 538) like Bernard-Lazare who had had the courage to publish "The Truth of the Dreyfus Affair" in 1896. Péguy paid touching tribute to this old friend who died at the age of thirty-eight.

Péguy was willing to accept Halévy's apology for the past provided that it was not the past of Péguy and his friends but was rather that of all those who had assured the decomposition of the Dreyfus mystique into politics. Péguy rightly saw the Affair as a religious crisis in which all the political force of the church was anti-Dreyfusite. This Jewish-Christian crisis became subsequently a crisis of the French mystique brought about by men like the anti-militarist writer Gustave Hervé and Jaurès. The latter bore the responsibility for causing the Affair to be thought of as anti-Christian and anti-French. Péguy's diatribe against these two men is virulent. He maintains that politics has denatured Socialism, by which he means his brand, his mystique of the Socialism of the harmonious city. Capitalist and bourgeois sabotage have also contributed to this corruption of Socialism, of "our Socialism," writes Péguy, which "was essentially and officially a general theory, a doctrine, a general method, a philosophy of the organization and re-organization of work, of the restoration of work" (pp. 592–3). Péguy does not seem to have tried to put his theory, doctrine, method, or philosophy into practice. He left that to others, then complained of the results.

The problem, according to him, was not one of science against religion but that the Christian world lacks charity. The spiritual poverty of Christianity has changed the mystique into politics. The church has become the official religion of the state bourgeoisie. Even the popular universities were an artificial creation of the intellectual party. The root of all evil is money, a concept on which Péguy has dwelt earlier and will dwell on again at great length. His idea is at least as old as the thirty pieces of silver and thus not particularly unique to the modern world. Péguy extolls the French tradition of generosity. So many are willing to exert "A full and sober, gay and discreet heroism, a heroism in the French manner" (p. 605). As much as I admire French generosity and heroism, I am not sure the French have a monopoly on either. Nevertheless, Jaurès and Hervé were, according to Péguy, responsible for the mortal blow to the belief in the innocence of Dreyfus while the Affair itself was in part the disastrous result of counterespionage, a system from which we are still suffering necessarily and unnecessarily today. Certainly Péguy made heroic efforts in behalf of Dreyfus, but he may not be really entitled to claim "We have sacrificed our entire life to him, since this affair has marked us for life" (p. 617). Dreyfus did not ask Péguy to sacrifice his life to his cause, nor can he be held responsible for Péguy's interest in the Affair. Péguy goes on to point out the anti-semitism rampant in Russia and Salonica as evidence of what was still happening to the Jewish race. Certainly Péguy raises a vigorous cry against anti-semitism but his reasons provoke serious reservations:

A great history, I say a great military history like the wars of the Revolution and the Empire can only be explained in this way: a sudden feeling of need, a very profound need for glory, for war, for history which at a given moment seizes a whole people, a whole race, and causes it to explode, to erupt. A mysterious need of an inscription. Historical. A mysterious need of a sort of historical fecundity. A mysterious need of inscribing a great history in eternal history. Any other explanation is vain, reasonable, rational, sterile, unreal. In

the same way our Dreyfus Affair can only be explained by a need,
the same, by a need for heroism that seized a whole generation,
ours, by a need for war, for a military war, and for military glory,
by a need for sacrifice and even martyrdom, perhaps, (undoubtedly),
by a need for saintliness. (p. 643)

Péguy's reasoning is dubious if not specious and suspect. In any
event, he had World War I in which to make it all come true.

Péguy wrote at length of his own poverty. Attention to this
subject may be another aspect of his own mystique, of his concept of martyrdom. He was a bad businessman who chose to
ignore the rules of good business in the name of his mystique.
Certainly there is a difference in kind between the martyrdom
of Joan of Arc and that of Péguy. As opposed to Péguy, Halévy
was a relatively well-to-do man who perhaps knew he was a
bad businessman and thus was a good enough businessman to
refuse the directorship of the *Cahiers* that Péguy begged him
to accept in 1903. These differences must have played some
part in Péguy's desire to dissociate his past from the apology
Halévy was making for his. Péguy repeats the idea he had
expressed in "Concerning Jean Coste" that a single injustice like
that of the Dreyfus Affair dishonored a whole nation. He also
writes briefly of his ideas on temporal and eternal death as
exemplified by the conversation between St. Louis and Joinville on leprosy and mortal sin, a subject to be treated at
greater length in *Le Mystère des saints Innocents* (*The Mystery
of the Holy Innocents*). He also repeats that everything we
do is translated and thus reduced into parliamentary political
language, a point he had already made in "Parliamentary Political Reprise." He concludes that his fifteen years of misery
and service to the republic have resulted in freedom of conscience for everyone except himself and other true republicans,
men who believed in something. Thus has he spent and mis-
spent his youth. Daniel Halévy, the butt of the essay, has the
generosity to call it "one of Péguy's finest pieces of writing."[2]
A more recent critic writes that "Of all the great writings in
prose, 'Our Youth' is by far the most controlled, the tightest
in its demonstration. Péguy holds himself severely in check,
careful not to wound, passionately desirous of convincing and

even of seducing."[3] Jaurès may not have been wounded but Halévy certainly was, as we shall see. In the essay Péguy claimed a great deal for himself while putting clearly into words the dilemma of his generation.

V *An Apology*

Not unnaturally, Halévy was somewhat upset by Péguy's remarks. Péguy published his apology in "Victor-Marie, comte Hugo, *Solvuntur objecta*" (Victor-Marie, Count Hugo, *Solvuntur objecta*, pp. 661–840) in October 1910. Here Péguy asserts that he had never insulted anyone except "very dangerous public enemies" (p. 662). The misunderstanding between Halévy and himself stems from the fact that they belonged to different classes, Halévy to the "old liberal bourgeois republican Orleanist tradition" while Péguy was a peasant (p. 668). Péguy's greatest hope had been to become a university professor but he had failed and could now only repeat, "Forty is a terrible age" (p. 669). Repeating an idea expressed in "Clio," Péguy feels that no man can be called happy as long as he is not dead. He is still peasant enough to be uneasy in a salon. He would have liked to live in the fifteenth century for he could have fought well with the arms of the time. A peasant can only become an unsuccessful bourgeois while losing his being as an authentic peasant. Péguy perhaps never defined his own social condition more clearly. He was never a complete bourgeois, but he was no longer a true peasant. While giving his readers an amusing and informative lesson in peasant dialect, Péguy asserts that irony is contrary to peasant speech and even to the French genius. As a result, the words he had spoken as a peasant were mistaken for irony by the bourgeois Halévy.

The number forty was a mystical one for Péguy. He noted that forty years separated Hugo's poems in *Châtiments* (*Punishments*) on the Battle of Waterloo from the battle itself while forty years separated Péguy, Halévy, and their generation from the Franco-Prussian War. During their sylvan rambles they quoted Hugo endlessly, as well as Corneille and Racine. Hugo, being the pagan genius he was, was the only poet to give us in his poem "Booz endormi" a pagan and Jewish view of the incarnation which was, as Péguy had said in "Veronica," the insertion of the eternal in the temporal, the spiritual in the carnal. Péguy also observes that Hugo never reworked his publications but allowed one work to correct another, which was pretty much Péguy's method of operation in general, and more specifically in the present essay.

Returning to the subject of generations, Péguy notes that parents want their children's lives to be a prolongation of theirs. He counsels that if we let children do their own calculating, they will eliminate the earlier generation and lead their own lives. Recalling his dictum "We are vanquished," Péguy also returns to his old enemy the Sorbonne, which had fallen into the scholastics of materialism. After ten pages on the subject Péguy points out that he has not thought to judge Halévy or his courage. He can only excuse himself and his lapse as the result of fatigue. The question of who suffered the most is a moot one. Like Ernest Psichari, the grandson of Renan who served in the colonial artillery, Halévy and Péguy know that peace can only be maintained by force. Halévy had been opposed to Barrès but Péguy quotes the latter's ideas on the Romantic as opposed to the Classic, a subject Péguy had explored in "Concerning Jean Coste." Barrès states that the sentiment called Romantic, if it is led to a higher degree of culture, takes on a Classical character. Péguy will create two parties of which Halévy will belong to the second, that of the forty year-olds whose first principle will be that they shall never have "any more triumphant mornings" (p. 840).

The essay is thus a strange sort of apology in which Péguy asks for forgiveness in such a way as to seem to put Halévy in the wrong and talks much more about Hugo than Halévy and almost as much about Psichari as Halévy. Although he invited Halévy to continue contributing to the *Cahiers*, Halévy switched to another review and never again listed among his complete works those published by Péguy. He was, nevertheless, among the earliest to write about Péguy in his *Quelques nouveaux maîtres (Some New Masters)* of 1914. The irony is that Halévy is only remembered today first as a man about whom Péguy wrote; second as a man who published a book on *Péguy et les "Cahiers de la Quinzaine"*; third as the son of the famous

librettist, Ludovic Halévy. In the conclusion to his book on
Péguy, Halévy writes, "Péguy has his dour moments; he has
candour too. May he be loved for the one, pitied for the
other."[4] Halévy may have forgiven, but he had not forgotten.

CHAPTER 5

The Catholic Pamphleteer: 1910–1914

IN "Les Amis des Cahiers" (The Friends of the *Cahiers*)[1] of November 1910, Péguy repeats his pleas published in "To Our Friends, To Our Subscribers" of 1909 and adds details from "We Are the Vanquished" which he had not published. Péguy had not publicly asked all collaborators to subscribe to the *Cahiers,* but he does so now. Publishing such an idea does not make it any more sound. Péguy's enemies were no longer limited to Paris. They were turning up as far away as Lyon. The subscribers may have been tiring of Péguy's endless account of his tribulations. He accomplished an Herculean task, but no one had asked him to do it. He certainly did not realize the irony of telling his subscribers that they had only been promised a review of seventy-two pages and were being given a review that averaged one hundred forty-four pages, particularly since the last issue ran to two hundred sixty-eight pages and was his own "Victor-Marie, Count Hugo." The subscribers may not have known they were subscribing to quite so much Péguy. But Péguy also admits publicly that he has ruined himself and his family, a fact he had not published. He complains again about the enormous budgets of the Bulletin of the League of Rights and *L'Humanité.* One good point he makes is to ask subscribers to take out an additional subscription for a French or a foreign university. Aside from that his plea is not very appealing.

In "OEuvres choisies de Charles Péguy of 1900–1910)" (Selected Works of Charles Péguy 1900–1910, pp. 859–76) of June 1911, Péguy expresses his gratitude to the editor of his works, his old friend Charles-Lucas de Peslouan, to his new friend the publisher Bernard Grasset, to his old friend and fellow-worker André Bourgeois who drew up the bibliography, and to the painter and son of an old friend, Pierre Laurens, for the portrait

74

that heads the volume. Pesloüan has in fact, by excerpting and rearranging Péguy's works, given them an order and a logic they did not have upon first publication and which they have not had since. Péguy himself was simply advertising his own work in the *Cahiers* as he had done for many other friends and collaborators. It is certainly one of Péguy's most gracious statements and perhaps one of the most gracious expressions of appreciation in French literature.

This graciousness resulted in part from Péguy's decision not to publish the last sixteen pages of his article. Under the title "Il me plaît . . ." (I Am Pleased . . . , pp. 879–94) they have been published posthumously and reveal the Péguy we have come to know. In them he relates the details of the sordid affair of the Academy's grand prize for literature that have been outlined in the biography of the first chapter. Strangely enough Péguy numbers the paragraphs beginning with eighty-six as if they were a continuation of "Victor-Marie, Count Hugo." In the first he attacks a certain Madame Cruppi whose political salon was against Péguy. Paragraph eighty-seven is devoted to Louis Barthou who is remembered today primarily because he was assassinated along with Alexander I of Yugoslavia in 1934. Péguy is puzzled why this man to whom he had done nothing was his declared enemy. Péguy's real goal was Ernest Lavisse. His naiveté in asking Lavisse, even through an intermediary, to remain neutral in his voting in the Academy after Péguy's violent attacks on him, no matter how much or little they were deserved, remains inconceivable today. That Péguy expected Lavisse to do anything but work energetically against him reveals Péguy's astonishing lack of perception. Péguy did not publish these sixteen pages. He rectified his error by publishing two hundred one pages on the subject the following September.

I *The New Theologians*

A certain François Le Grix published an article in the *Revue hebdomadaire* (*Weekly Review*) severely criticizing Péguy's *Mystère de la charité de Jeanne d'Arc*. Péguy replied by attacking the journal's editor Fernand Laudet in "Un nouveau théologien M. Fernand Laudet" (A New Theologian, Mr. Fernand Laudet, pp. 897–1097) in September 1911. Péguy's point of departure is weak if not totally indefensible: "one will never be able to undertake to ruin his [Péguy's] *Mystère* without condemning himself in so doing to undertake to ruin, in his work, the very foundations of our faith" (p. 897). A critic could not annihilate Péguy's *Mystère* without ruining the foundations of Péguy's peculiar brand of faith. A critic could, however, annihilate it without ever touching the foundations of faith in general. Péguy begins again with paragraph eighty-six, finding a connection in his own mind between this essay and his "Victor-Marie, Count Hugo" that escapes his readers.

Le Grix committed, nevertheless, several serious errors. He accused Péguy of not having consulted the documents in Joan's case. Péguy had read his Quicherat, Michelet, and several others. Le Grix also maintained that Péguy preferred the legendary Joan to the historical, the supernatural and saintly Joan to the missionary and martyr, claiming that only the Jesus of the last three years of his life belonged to us. With relish, Péguy demolished the argument about Jesus easily at length. Péguy's defense of the analogy with Joan is less convincing. The historical Joan is infinitely more interesting. Péguy was free to believe her supernatural and saintly. To prove it is impossible, of course, unless one already believes it. Péguy also drags out his argument about the rich and the poor and religion again, which proves nothing, and states categorically that "The people alone guarantee the saint" (p. 937). Péguy was in his own view both poor and of the people.

The insult that stung Péguy the deepest was, however, the use of his own favorite pejorative adjective "modern" against him. Everyone knows that there is no good modernism so Péguy could not help but be insulted. Péguy was convinced that Le Grix found all believers to be imbeciles. In defense of believers Péguy went so far as to praise worldly Catholicism, which sounds strange in view of his frequent condemnation of contemporary church politics. Nevertheless, Péguy approved only of a healthy revolutionary atheism, not of the reactionary bourgeois atheism he found on all sides. Unfortunately, Péguy also wanted to argue about Joan's voices. Again one is free to believe that they were divinely inspired, but one cannot prove it.

Le Grix also made the mistake of using the cliché "the age of faith" which anyone could demolish and which Péguy did with a vengeance. While catching his breath Péguy again extolls his old friend Bernard-Lazare, again complains of how his generation had been mistreated by the preceding generation, and makes the dubious observation that "man is never free except in the regiment" (p. 988). Péguy then insults Ernest Lavisse, the director of the *Revue critique,* Rudler, and Gustave Lanson again, and relives the period of the first *Cahiers* when he was "without a penny, sick, betrayed, abandoned on all sides" (p. 1007). As one critic puts it, Péguy suffered from "the complex of the poor."[2] He defends again his brand of mystical Socialism that he claims is closely related to Christianity, "a religion of poverty" (p. 1032). Péguy's brand of mystical Socialism is not very orthodox and his Socialist Catholicism is even less so. That he believed them to be closely related was his right, however.

Péguy's distinction between the ironic and the comic is not terribly clear either. He had already expressed his disdain of irony in "Victor-Marie, Count-Hugo" but in reading his works one finds very little that is funny and a great deal that is ironic. Only occasionally does Péguy rise to the classic heights of the comic and that most frequently when he is talking about himself which ends up by being tragic. The more Péguy writes, the more he repeats himself; the more he nears 1914, the more hysterical he seems to become, the more paranoid he sounds, the less he seems to be in control of what he is writing. In the end he does sound as if he takes himself for a fifth gospel, right after Matthew, Mark, Luke, and John. He does, and he gives one the impression that he has a unique corner on religion and morality and is free to preach to one and all. Only his sincere desire to be a chronicler whose master was Joinville saves him from being a complete bore, but when he says he has chosen Joan of Arc for his model, the reader again has serious doubts about Péguy's unstated, unavowed, and perhaps unconscious goal. All martyrdom is not necessarily good. While again praising Joinville as the chronicler of St. Louis, Péguy defends the Latin of the Vulgate against French translations. His argument is weakened by the fact that the Vulgate is itself a "Latin version"

of other texts. Péguy begins to sound more and more desperate
and as he does so, what he says becomes less and less meaningful. The modern reader would be hard put to choose between
Laudet and Péguy as new theologians.

II *Money and More Money*

The first two-thirds of Péguy's essay entitled "L'Argent"
(Money, pp. 1101–62) of February 1913 is a continuation of his
posthumous autobiographical sketch "Pierre, The Beginnings of
a Bourgeois Life." The article on the history of primary education since 1880 being introduced by Péguy had been written
by Théodore Naudy, the man who had insisted that Péguy
transfer from the pre-professional to the academic program.
Thus Péguy felt he owed a great deal of what he had become to
his former mentor.

Starting again from the more or less psychologically sound
major premise that all is decided by the time the child is twelve,
Péguy proceeds to draw a picture of "ancient France" before
1880, a view by a forty year old who looks at his youth through
rose-colored glasses. Péguy is historically accurate in maintaining that it was the period of the ascendance of the bourgeoisie,
but most analysts would mark its origins at a much earlier date.
Sartre, for example, places it at least as early as 1848 in "Qu'est-ce
que la littérature?" (What Is Literature). According to Péguy
everyone has become a member of the bourgeoisie and what is
worse, the bourgeoisie of money. From this phenomenon, he
derives the title of his essay. The reader becomes skeptical
when Péguy asserts that "In my time everyone sang" (p. 1105),
that everyone wanted to work, that everyone believed that "to
work was to pray" (p. 1108), that one earned nothing, lived on
nothing, and was happy. The economic strangulation may well
have been created by an intellectual bourgeois demagogy that
was the source of all modern ills. The Socialist political party
was composed entirely of bourgeois intellectuals while the Socialist syndicalist party was infested and infected with the same
political, intellectual, and bourgeois elements. The man to blame
for it all was, of course, Jaurès. He had betrayed Socialism to
the benefit of the bourgeois parties and Dreyfusism for reasons

of state. Now in his ardent pacifism he was betraying France itself to the benefit of German politics. Péguy with his conservative not to say reactionary Socialism could not condone the "modern" strikes that had not existed in his youth. In 1880 the enemy was still the Prussians; in 1913 the enemy was again the Prussians.

As a child Péguy had imbibed two diametrically opposed metaphysics, the scholarly, scientific, materialist, positivist metaphysics of progress taught by his schoolmasters and the metaphysics of the catechism imparted by the curates. He no longer believed at all in the former while believing with all his being in the latter. But, and what Péguy has to say next reveals a great deal about himself, it was the schoolmasters who captured and retained the heart and the confidence of their students while the curates were not very successful at these endeavors. Fundamentally the schoolmasters and curates were teaching the same moral lesson, the work ethic. But then Péguy went on to extol "the virtues of poverty" (p. 1127), although even poverty turned out to be unfaithful. "The reign of money" had begun, but for the first time Péguy was honest enough to admit that it had always ruled. His generation was agan the "sacrificed" generation, overwhelmed by a modernism that created the Lavisses and Laudets of this world who believed in nothing. Péguy wanted teachers to stick to teaching reading, writing, and arithmetic and to stay out of politics, forgetting that all of us live in a political world, even the teachers in their so-called ivory towers. Péguy again could not make the practice conform to his ideal. He concludes that the two plagues of the modern world are politics and alcohol and there he is probably right. We can't live without the one and won't live without the other.

The last third of Péguy's essay is his reply to a vicious review of his *OEuvres choisies* by Charles-Victor Langlois, a medievalist at the Sorbonne and subsequently director of the National Archives. Péguy made the mistake of printing the review in its entirety, for much of what Langlois says about both Péguy's style and personality as revealed in his published works is true. Admittedly Langlois was frequently petty but Péguy's defense is not very convincing. He accuses Langlois of accusing him of openly revealing his return to Catholicism in order to make his

literary and financial fortune. Langlois says nothing about
Péguy's return to Catholicism but he does accuse him unjustly
of writing about Joan of Arc in order to profit as a writer from
a contemporary literary fad. Whatever Langlois implies about
financial gain is certainly implicit rather than explicit, but it
was sufficient reason for Péguy to be able to fit this last third
of his essay into its title. His long diatribe against Lavisse has
less than nothing to do with Langlois' article. The reader is
again astounded at Péguy's naiveté in wondering what could
possibly explain "the tone of this article" (p. 1154). Péguy had
only to reread his own essays to find the real explanation for its
tone. But Péguy was merely being "comic" in asking the question. Actually he was being ironic, for the reason he dreamed
up was not even funny. The rest of his defense does not merit
comment. Péguy never learned the lesson Proust stated so well:
"The pamphleteer involuntarily shares his reputation with the
scoundrel he is denouncing."[3]

   Two months later Péguy published "L'Argent suite" (Money,
A Sequel, pp. 1165–1311) a one hundred forty seven page continuation of the preceding essay. He had found a review by
Rudler of a book by Lanson in the same issue of the *Revue
hebdomadaire* in which Langlois' article had appeared. In
addition to scolding Rudler for writing such a flattering review
of a book by his own teacher, Péguy gives him a lesson in
French grammar. He also deduces from the review that Lanson
in his account of a three months' visit to the United States has
obviously not adhered to the famous "method" according to
which he should have consulted all the literature and every
document on America before writing. Then Péguy sketches the
"parallel lives" of Charles Andler and Lanson, noting that only
Andler has remained faithful to the method and therefore might
never publish a book. Lanson's case is quite different. He spent
his life in secondary teaching until the age of forty when he was
named to the École Normale Supérieure. Péguy had been a
student in his course on the French theater and could not forgive
Lanson for his complete misunderstanding and mishandling of
Corneille.

   Lanson's second grave fault was to abandon his old master
Ferdinand Brunetière when the latter was to be named to the

Sorbonne. As a result of chicanery while Ernest Lavisse was director of the École Normale, everyone but Joseph Bédier left Brunetière to his fate. After twenty years in secondary teaching and fifteen years at the university, Lanson has now become a journalist, his third mistake according to Péguy. Lanson published regularly in the *Grande Revue* (*Great Review*), which was acceptable, but he also published regularly in the newspaper *Le Matin* (Morning) where his articles appeared on the women's page or among the classified advertisements, a situation that was an insult to the Sorbonne and to all intellectuals.

After noting that the sociologist Émile Durkheim was not a professor of philosophy but a professor against philosophy, Péguy again blamed Lanson for publishing literary and theater criticism once a week in *Le Matin* and once every two weeks in the *Grande Revue* because it meant that Lanson could not possibly adhere to his "scientific" method, even though he was being much more pleasant, particularly with the members of the Academy. From that point on Péguy loses all sense of proportion. He rails against the "debunkers" of history like Langlois and Charles Babut who are disturbing the order of "God, the church, France, the army, the customs, [and] the laws" (p. 1201). He criticizes Ernest Lavisse's betrayal of all parties, and Lucien Herr's fanaticism. He accuses them all, including Jaurès, of playing into the hands of the German menace. In trying to alert the French to the danger, Péguy goes so far as to say that "The military structure is the temporal cradle in which customs and laws and the arts and even religion and language and race are able . . . to go to bed in order to grow," since "the temporal is essentially military" (p. 1218). Péguy had published numerous articles on oppressed peoples including those of the French Congo but he saw no contradiction in writing that thanks to the soldier, French was spoken in Paris as well as "from Dakar to Bizerte" (p. 1224). His attack against the pacifists led him to write that "War has charms [*douceurs*] comparable to no other" (p. 1226).

He recounts the street fights against the anti-semites when they invaded the Sorbonne in 1897 during the Dreyfus Affair. It is interesting to speculate on which side he would have found himself in 1968. He excoriates the historian Charles Seignobos because he had guaranteed in a German newspaper that "there will be no war, because war destroys the armies" (p. 1230). He did not want a repetition of 1870, and while violent anti-militarists like Hervé heightened the possibility, at least Hervé was an honest antimilitarist. Péguy condemned Francis de Pressensé, President of the League of the Rights of Man, because of his attitude toward the problem of Alsace-Lorraine, the provinces taken by the Germans in the treaty ending the Franco-Prussian War. Péguy claims that the politics of the guillotine of the National Convention during the Revolution "[are] pacifist politics and humanitarian politics. [They are the politics] that cost the least. [They are the politics] that spare the most. [They are the politics] that are least costly, both in men and in money" (p. 1241). In short, they are "Jaurès in a tumbril" (p. 1240). Péguy could not know that Jaurès would be assassinated just one month and five days before he himself died.

Peguy's religious patriotism left no place for the religious pacifist, the conscientious objector, because it was a contradiction in terms. If one is religious, one is patriotic. If one is patriotic, one is religious. According to Péguy, "Dreyfusism . . . was a system of absolute liberty, of absolute truth, of absolute justice, and of a profound spiritual order" (pp. 1259–60). Profound and spiritual it certainly was but all those "absolutes" make one wonder how human it was. Sounding like a broken record, Péguy returns to money, "the only master and God" (p. 1267); then to his concept of "the insertion of the spiritual in the carnal and the insertion of the eternal in the temporal" (p. 1271); and finally to his "sacrificed" generation, "constantly betrayed by our masters and our leaders" (p. 1297). Péguy does have the good grace to quote a review by Gustave Lanson in which he takes exactly the same view of Alsace-Lorraine as Péguy. He concludes by stating: "It is perfectly obvious that we are taking part in events the likes of which have never been seen and that we have the impression that we are going to tumble over events of an unprecedented magnitude" (p. 1309). In April 1913 Péguy saw clearly what was coming in August 1914. The tragedy is that his penetrating vision was obscured by so much reckless and useless verbiage.

III   *Bergson, Descartes, and Victor Hugo*

As a reply to the negative criticism of Bergson's philosophy by Julien Benda that appeared in the *Cahiers* in November 1913, Péguy published his "Note sur M. Bergson et la philosophie bergsonienne" (Note on Mr. Bergson and the Bergsonian Philosophy, pp. 1315–47) in April 1914. His essay is more an appreciation of Bergsonism or a "prayer for the good use of Bergsonism" than an analysis. Actually, only the first fourth of the article is devoted strictly to Bergson. The major portion is reserved for Descartes while in the concluding pages Péguy speaks of both Descartes and Bergson and of philosophy in general. He begins by stating that Bergsonism was an attempt to bring about an internal revolution in reason, wisdom, logic, and intelligence; thus "Bergsonism is not at all a geography, it is a geology" (p. 1315). He also observes that the real revolution of Bergsonism was an attempt at a certain re-situation of thought in the face of the parallel realities of the vegetable and animal kingdoms, of thought and being. He wanted to refute Benda's designation of Bergsonism as a philosophy of the pathetic (*pathétique*, pp. 1316–7) by demonstrating that it was the "denunciation of a universal intellectualism, that is to say of a universal laziness that consists of always using the ready-made [*tout fait*]" as opposed to the "making itself" (*se faisant*, pp. 1322–3). Bergsonism also proved that creation, as it moves from the future to the past through the intermediary of the present, changes not only time but also being and the nature of being.

If Cartesianism was essentially a denunciation of disorder, then Bergsonism was essentially a denunciation of the ready-made. Thus Cartesianism was a philosophy of order and Bergsonism a philosophy of reality. Péguy realises that he is "only a poor moralist" (p. 1344) but he is convinced that "a great philosophy is not at all one that settles questions once and for all but one that asks them." "A great philosophy is not one that pronounces definitive judgments, that furnishes a definitive truth. It is one that introduces a disquietude, that creates a disturbance" (p. 1338). Bergsonism was, in the end, "an effort to conduct reason within the grip of reality" (p. 1343). Thus Péguy was able to write a sincere and intelligent appreciation of an old friend and his philosophy without insulting anyone. Péguy had obviously forgiven Bergson for not writing the introduction to his *OEuvres choisies*. He used Descartes to defend Bergson precisely because Bergson's enemies were using Descartes to attack him, thus the long and only apparent digressions on the earlier philosopher.

Péguy's posthumous "Note conjointe sur Victor Hugo" (Added Note on Victor Hugo, pp. 1351-5) was not literary criticism but a brief meditation on the poet's career. Returning to his distinction between Classic and Romantic, Péguy insists that not even Homer was as profoundly classic as Hugo. Romanticism was merely a malady that Hugo wanted to give himself but which never took. Returning also to his distinction between genius and talent, the temporal and the spiritual, the secular and the eternal, Péguy claims that Hugo's great displays were the result of his genius, his reticences the result of his immense but weak talent. No man can pursue at the same time his career and his work, happiness and salvation. Hugo's whole career can be explained by his terrible fear of not succeeding in his temporal career. Instead of realizing that he was the greatest classical genius since Corneille and one of the greatest geniuses the world has ever seen, Hugo worked only towards making himself a greater man than anyone else. By the time Hugo arrived on the scene in 1820, the glories of France were but a memory. All that remained was an intellectual Paris and an intellectual France that resulted in the third-hand intellectual Egypt of *Les Orientales*. Hugo is certainly France's greatest poet but as a genius he was no Homer, Dante, Shakespeare, Cervantes, or Goethe. Péguy's superlatives constantly compel him to claim more than he can prove. Péguy's literary criticism of Hugo will be discussed at greater length later.

The essay Péguy so dramatically left unfinished on his desk August 1, 1914, when the call to arms came, was the "Note conjointe sur M. Descartes et la philosophie cartésienne" (Added Note on Mr. Descartes and the Cartesian Philosophy, pp. 1359–1554), one of his longest. Actually Péguy spends only two scant pages on Descartes and they seem to reflect a misreading of Descartes. When Descartes wrote that he attempted to find the first causes of everything and then examined the first and most ordinary effects of these causes, he concluded by saying "and it seems to me that thereby I found the heavens." I have always interpreted the verb "found" in the sense that Descartes, by his method of reasoning, "was led to" or "came upon" the heavens. Péguy interprets it as "discovered" in the sense that Columbus discovered America. I doubt that this was Descartes' meaning. Be that as it may, Péguy set out for a walk in the Latin Quarter with his old friend Julien Benda. Benda was "the only adversary of Bergson who knew what it was all about" (pp. 1353-4). The friendship between Péguy and Benda was so profound that Péguy could write that "to love is to say that the loved one is right when he is wrong" (p. 1365). In discussing their similarities Péguy asserts that they both knew that "there have never been but two successes in the world," the ancient Greek and the modern French. In discussing their differences, Péguy notes that every Jew proceeds from a certain oriental fatalism while every living French Christian proceeds from a certain occidental revolt. The Christian (Péguy?) is still foolish enough "not to have ceased hoping secretly that in sacrificing happiness he would at least have his work" (p. 1373), while Péguy is convinced that he will have neither. Where cultures are concerned Péguy notes that "the Jew is a man who has always read, the Protestant a man who has read since Calvin, the Catholic is a man who has read since Ferry" (p. 1377). Jules Ferry is the man who was successful in bringing about free and compulsory lay education in France in 1882.

Péguy verbally leaves Benda standing on the Boulevard Saint-Germain much as Jaurès had literally left him standing on the street many years earlier, and returns to him only once. Speaking of his race, Péguy mentions again that he only wanted to be "a sinner of the most ordinary species" (p. 1380). Noting that "every modern man is a miserable newspaper" (p. 1383), he recounts again his grandmother's illiteracy and analyzes the operation of grace. Romain Rolland calls his account "a curious and indiscreet analysis of the mechanics of grace,"[4] for Péguy compares them to the physics of hydrostatics and concludes that "One is always weighable. One is not always penetrable" (p. 1391).

Returning to his favorite play, Péguy reveals much about the relationship between Polyeucte and Sévère that remains sensitive and nuanced. However, he asserts that the Bergsonian system taught us that "the death of a being is its fulfilling of habit, its fulfilling of memory, that is to say its fulfilling of aging" (p. 1400). Hope remains the greatest virtue, according to Péguy, and hope remained Péguy's greatest virtue. The positivists, materialists, and determinists fought Bergson, the man who had reintroduced liberty into the world and rescued France from intellectual German servitude. The reactionary politicians of the *Action française* and the politicans of the spiritual life were against Bergson, for he had just been placed on the Index. Péguy knew it was a tragedy because Platonic, Cartesian, and Bergsonian thought were the fruits of the earth that we store in our cellars and barns. Dedicating many more pages to his favorite subjects, Corneille, to whom I shall return later, Joan of Arc, and St. Louis, Péguy reminds us that *Le Cid* is not a conflict between love and duty but a conflict between one grandeur and another, between love and honor. Speaking of Sévère in *Polyeucte*, Péguy again asserts that pagan antiquity, ancient and pagan humanity itself was "a temple of purity" (p. 1449).

Péguy wrote much about Bergson that is still pertinent, particularly on the subject of our mistaken view of the "historical present." Yet, according to Péguy, Benjamin Franklin was guilty of encouraging the idea of the savings bank, thus leading everyone to sacrifice the present to the future. All anyone can think about is saving for retirement so that the question becomes one of knowing "if the world is destined to become an immense asylum of old people" (p. 1496). If his reasoning was not quite correct, Péguy nevertheless foresaw the problem of advancing age in the Western World as it is today. The more Péguy writes, the more the reader becomes convinced that he himself has no intention of growing old. He was so depressed by "the reign of money" (p. 1502) that he took refuge in writing, about Bergson and the present repeatedly, comparing the Bergsonian maneuver to the Napoleonic, insisting that "Bergson, and no other, liberated us from this metaphysics of the modern world that tried to offer itself as a physics" (p. 1539).[5] Péguy's metaphysics are his own brand of Catholicism which he describes in the concluding pages of this unfinished essay. He finds his joy to be that of the Catholic who does not, like the Protestant, erect road signs but who uses the one he already has, the cross.

Péguy seemed to be writing without thinking, or writing in order not to think. How else can one explain remarks that include "the most beautiful verses are those that come of themselves" (p. 1367). One wonders how many poets would agree. By now the reader is accustomed to Péguy's superlatives. However, statements of praise like: "*Polyeucte* was the greatest and most perfect work that one will ever see" (p. 1393) and Molière was "the greatest comic genius who has ever appeared in the world" (p. 1443) produce an effect opposite to that which Péguy intends. Péguy's biggest blooper occurs when he notes that what was most important to Rodrigue and Don Gormas in *Le Cid* was that the duel take place and take place according to the rules: "Gormas dead was as convinced of it as Rodrigue living" (p. 1422). I am not sure just what Gormas could be convinced of once he was dead. Péguy was trapped by his own antithesis but pin-pointing such lapses is easy for the reader. The editor Péguy was in dire need of a good and very critical editor himself, but it is too late to cry over all that spilled ink.

CHAPTER 6

The Poet: 1897–1912

PÉGUY published his first poetic work, a dramatic trilogy called *Jeanne d'Arc* (*Joan of Arc*),[1] late in 1897 at the age of twenty-four. Because the dedication is signed Marcel and Pierre Baudouin, the latter being Péguy's early pseudonym, while the last act concludes with "completed by Pierre Baudouin," we assume the attribution to be Péguy's salute to the inspiration provided by his late friend. The three plays, *A Domremy* (*At Domremy*), *Les Batailles* (*The Battles*), and *Rouen*, comprise eight parts divided into twenty-four acts, more nearly what we should call eight acts and twenty-four scenes that vary greatly in length. The plays include sixty characters in addition to Joan plus at least forty non-speaking roles. The trilogy covers the years 1425–1431 of Joan's life from the age of thirteen to her death at nineteen. Wagnerian in scope, the plays would require three evenings to perform.

The modern reader finds the dedication to "the universal socialist Republic" difficult to reconcile with a play on the subject of Joan of Arc. Her role in the rise of French nationalism brought with it little that was universal and even less that was Socialist or republican. Her devout faith was at odds both with Péguy's rejection of religion, which probably took place as early as 1891, and with his adherence to Socialism in 1894 or 1895. Yet Joan's faith that failed to conform to the norms of the establishment would coincide later both with Péguy's return to a religion unacceptable to the church and with his adherence to a Socialism unacceptable to the party. One critic explains Joan this way: "In the beginning were the republic of the lay school, the classical humanities of the lycée [high school], and the Socialism of the Rue d'Ulm. Joan of Arc was the synthesis."[2] The Rue d'Ulm was the address of the

Collège de France. Another critic puts it this way: "Its [the play's] historical symbolism, presented moreover in the direct reality of the facts of the past, is valid as a Socialist demonstration."[3] If the problem of the source of the religious inspiration for the play remains to plague the scholar, fervent patriotism in all its forms was a constant among Péguy's preoccupations.

The trilogies of Sophocles may well have suggested to Péguy the form his play was to take. His historical sources included the *Jeanne d'Arc* of Michelet[4] as well as that of Henri Wallon[5] and both the *Aperçus* of Quicherat[6] and the five volumes of his edition of the *Procès*. While Péguy created at least one character and switched a role or two in the trial, he remained generally faithful to the historical truth as far as we know it. Today's reader is as puzzled by the great spaces and whole pages left blank by Péguy in the original edition as were the author's contemporaries. Péguy may have sought to offer his reader pause for thought or he may have already realized that this first work was only the skeleton to which he would add the flesh in a later work on the same subject. Thus the original edition covered seven hundred fifty-two pages while the three plays fit comfortably in just over three hundred in the Pléiade edition. Perhaps in spite of himself Péguy participated in the typographical experiments that extend in French literature from Rabelais to Butor and the "new new novelists." Péguy wrote the plays primarily in prose although once or twice he approached free verse, while the dramatic passages are in more or less regular alexandrines.

The theme of the plays, announced in the dedication and the first and second acts, is universal evil as evidenced by human suffering and war in this life, and by eternal damnation in the next. Eternal damnation was one of the tenets of Catholicism to which Péguy could not subscribe, let alone believe in. The story of Joan and her voices, her victories and her defeats, is too well known to need recounting here. Among Joan's voices was that of St. Michael. Late in the trilogy we learn from the English soldiers that they were fighting under the sign of St. George while the French were fighting under the sign of St. Michael. By such means Péguy gave stylistic unity to his three plays in addition to the historical unity of Joan's life. He used many similar devices. Joan's "Farewell to the Meuse" (*Adieu, Meuse...*, pp. 80–1), the river she loved so well in Lorraine, is, if not great poetry, a haunting piece of thirty-one lines worthy of almost any anthology even though one critic calls the lyric poetry "the weak part of the youthful work."[7] The soliloquy achieves added poignancy when Joan quotes it in her farewell to life near the end of the trilogy (p. 308). The lines are mingled with her musings on eternal damnation and thus the allusions to the earlier parts of the play are doubled. The effect is compounded because Joan is also repeating with slight variations the lines on the same subject spoken just a bit earlier by Guillaume Evrard, doctor of theology, and treasurer and canon of the cathedral of Langres (pp. 301–2). Péguy achieves the same effect by the repetition, again with slight variation, of a mere phrase, a simple yet compelling expression like "the strange love of absence" (*l'étrange amour d'absence*, p. 94)—that is, the strange love for a place or person that arises in the soul through absence. In the end when Joan is alone and facing death, without family or friends or her faithful companions, the phrase becomes "the strange exile of absence" (*L'étrange exil d'absence*, p. 312), the strange exile created by absence, the absence that is death.

Péguy also realizes superb irony by such repetitions. Joan demonstrates her faith in both her religion and her assigned task when she says "to work at a worthy task is simply another way of praying" (*travaillez à la bonne besogne, c'est encore de la prière*, p. 113). In the following act Joan compliments a soldier on a job well done in the battle the day before. He replies modestly that he was only "doing his job" (*c'est mon métier*), to which she answers, "It's my job too at present" (*Moi aussi, maître Jean, c'est mon métier, à présent*, p. 128). Such simple sincerity and dedication is transformed, in the grim scene between the torturer and the locksmith who manufactures his instruments when each is talking about his grisly profession, into the enormous cliché, "The main thing in life is that one do his job well" (*Enfin, le principal, dans la vie, c'est qu'on fasse bien son métier*, p. 286). Their point is that Joan should have stuck to the job of guarding her flocks.

Just as Joan refused to attend the war councils because the

advice conflicted with the dictates of her voices, so she refused to conduct war as every good soldier knows it should be conducted, by sparing no one. A hardened soldier called her "a woman who does not wish to bow to the necessities of life" (*C'est une femme qui ne veut pas se plier aux nécessités de la vie*, p. 156). Péguy throughout his life always seemed to heed only his own voices and certainly he characterized himself in Joan as a man who refused to bow to the necessities of life. Therein lay his strength and his weakness. If he appeared to take himself too seriously at times, he obviously delighted in showing how an endless series of conflicting views could all be proved by quoting from the Bible (pp. 181–99). While these pompous doctors of theology take themselves too seriously and exemplify the would-be intellectuals who lose themselves in the extremes of useless details, they also reveal Péguy's nascent anti-intellectualism. Although one must admit that Péguy in his way was one of the great intellectuals of the day who frequently lost both himself and his reader in the lengthy development of relatively useless details.

Péguy hoped that his trilogy would be performed, but in vain. The blank spaces in the published edition would be difficult to recreate in the theater except by silence and an empty stage. Given the numerous pauses indicated within and between the speeches, the plays would drag on mercilessly. With a touch of irony here and a bit of humor there, Péguy's first literary work, this "drama of intense spiritual despair,"[8] contains an occasional moving speech, now and again an effective scene, and patches of poignant poetry. "The prose is simple, clear, vigorous, familiar without vulgarity, exactly adapted to the rank, temperament, and profession of the characters"[9] and "without a single one of the traits, tics, and singularities that characterize both his psychological person and his literary genius."[10] If *Jeanne d'Arc* is no masterpiece, it does provide the point of departure for Péguy's future literary development. The best and the most that can be said of it is that the reader might well wish that all history be recounted in just such a fashion with its kings and battles, victories and defeats, heroes and heroines, moments of humor and pathos, revealed by the spoken word that creates character at the same time as action, recreates atmosphere as well as fact.

I *King Dagobert*

In 1903 Péguy published *La Chanson du roi Dagobert* (*The Song of King Dagobert*, pp. 327–62), again using the pseudonym Pierre Baudouin. Dagobert I ruled the Franks from 629–639. His goldsmith, treasurer, and intelligent advisor was the Bishop of Noyon, Eloi, later St. Eloi. In the dedication Péguy takes pride in his peasant ancestry: "To the memory of my grandmother, a peasant, who did not know how to read, and who was the first to teach me the French language" (p. 328). Thus the eighty jingles have as a point of departure not the great written tradition of French literature but the children's folksong *Le bon roi Dagobert*. The first twenty follow a fixed form: a couplet, a quatrain, and a couplet rhyming aa bbcc bb, the couplets composed of a hemistich and an octosyllable and the quatrains of five-syllable lines. Beginning with the twenty-first Péguy creates variations on the basic form.

The poems are meant to amuse and include such obvious puns as the proper name Fabert that becomes a number three Faber pencil (p. 346) as well as such homely problems as balancing the books of the *Cahiers* (p. 350) and local events like the balloon ascensions at annual festivals (p. 357). Péguy makes fun of the Romantic poets when he has his King Dagobert paraphrase Vigny's famous line, *Dieu, que le son du cor est triste au fond des bois* (God, but the sound of the horn is sad in the depths of the woods). Dagobert states flatly: "I like the sound of the horn at evening in the depths of the woods" (p. 356).

The light touch is not, however, Péguy's real forte. He could not resist ridiculing the lack of faith among the Parisians (p. 350):

Le bon roi Dagobert	The good king Dagobert
Voulait prêcher dans le désert	Wanted to preach in the desert
Comme le Baptiste;	Like the Baptist;
Le grand saint Eloi	The great St. Eloi
Lui dit: o mon roi,	Said to him: Oh my king,
Parlez à Paris	Speak in Paris

Emprès de Saint-Denis;	So near Saint-Denis;
C'est le plus grand désert	It is the greatest desert
Qu'ayons au royaume de France.	That we have in the kingdom of France.

In contrast, King Dagobert weeps at the death of Scheurer-Kestner, vice-president of the Senate and one of the earliest Dreyfusites. Nevertheless, Dagobert is happy that Scheurer-Kestner has not lived to see the political degradation of the spirit of Dreyfusism (p. 358). In his satire on parliamentary government Dagobert votes for Paul Doumer who was governor-general of Indochina from 1896 to 1902 (p. 359). Péguy could not have known that Doumer would indeed be elected president of France in 1931, only to be assassinated the following year. Dagobert also did not hesitate to poke fun at Umberto, king of Italy (p. 359). After eighty stanzas even Dagobert runs out of rhymes in *-ert* and his *Song* comes to an end, an unusual and somewhat amusing interlude in Péguy's literary production, if not a particularly important one.

II *The First Mystery*

Between *Jeanne d'Arc* of 1897 and *Le Mystère de la charité de Jeanne d'Arc* (*The Mystery of the Charity of Joan of Arc*, pp. 363–525) of 1910, Péguy announced his return to the Catholic faith in 1908. Adopting the form of the medieval mystery play, Péguy took the twenty pages of the first two acts of *Jeanne d'Arc* and expanded them into one hundred sixty as preparation for the celebration of the five hundredth anniversary of her birth in 1912. The play is dedicated to Marcel Baudouin and is written in a mixture of prose and free verse with only rarely a few alexandrines.

Most of the lines of *Jeanne d'Arc* are quoted practically without change and the basic theme with its attendant ideas remains the same. For example, Joan's friend Hauviette, a young girl of sound faith and lots of good sense, repeats Joan's idea from the earlier play that "To work is to pray" (*Travailler, c'est prier*, p. 374). More disturbing, however, is her repetition of her own remark, "in order to kill war, you have to make war" (*Mais pour tuer la guerre, il faut faire la guerre,* pp. 33 and 393). This attitude may have existed in the time of Joan but somehow it has the ring of pre-World War I. Certainly World War II, the Korean War, the Algerian War, and the Vietnam War have not proved the axiom. It lies, however, at the heart of Joan's dilemma.

Joan seeks the advice of a nun, Madame Gervaise. In their conversation Joan returns to the theme of absence but from the opposite point of view. This time she feels that "*All* those whom I loved are absent from me" (Tous *ceux que j'aimais sont absents de moi,* p. 424), even God. She now knows that her difference has isolated and exiled all others, including God, from her because she must cause suffering in order to eliminate it. Madame Gervaise, in her attempt to guide and console Joan, maintains that "There is a useful suffering" (*Il y a une souffrance utile,* p. 431). I am not convinced that human suffering can ever be useful, no matter how great the cause. Madame Gervaise is trying, however, to draw an analogy between the Passion of Christ and the charity for mankind it exemplified and Joan's humble, earthly task. Unfortunately, Madame Gervaise takes almost fifty pages to recount the Passion in free verse and while many of the passages are moving, the Bible tells a better story. Although Madame Gervaise states unequivocally in her conclusion that "we must not make war" (*il ne faut pas faire la guerre,* p. 490), she also says that "we must try with all our human strength to suffer as best we can, and even to the utmost suffering without ever killing ourselves ... if we truly do not wish in our cowardice to allow others to be damned" (*nous devons tâcher de toutes nos forces humaines à souffrir du mieux que nous pouvons, et jusqu'à la souffrance extrême sans nous tuer jamais ... si vraiment nous ne voulons pas lâchement laisser damner les autres,* p. 519), and ourselves along with them. While this concept is perhaps orthodox, it weakens the impact of Péguy's message.

The reader is surprised to note that in the middle of a prose passage, Péguy suddenly falls into alexandrines: *Heureux ceux qui buvaient le regard de vos yeux; heureux ceux qui mangeaient le pain de votre table ... Hereux ceux qui buvaient le lait de vos paroles* (Happy those who drank the glance of your eyes; happy those who ate the bread of your table ... Happy those who drank the milk of your words, p. 409). The formula of the "beatitude" (p. 519) is the famous one that Péguy will use in his *Eve* in 1913.

Péguy's first *Mystère* is a compelling exploration of religious faith, a passionate analysis of human suffering, and a courageous revolt against inevitable and eternal damnation. Certain passages read aloud are truly moving. But great religious literature is not necessarily great literature. To be great, religious literature must reveal a faith that is more than a faith in faith. Spiritual faith can be beautiful but a specific faith must be generalized so that it reveals somewhere a faith in others, a faith of which Péguy frequently seemed incapable and a faith that is not found in one line of his *Mystère*. Just when Péguy's vision seems to have closed in upon us, he opens it up with the magnificent concluding line, *Orléans, qui êtes au pays de Loire* (Orleans, you who are in the country of the Loire, p. 525), and miraculously all of Joan's future lies before the reader, her faith in herself and in her companions, the faith she aroused in others, her victories, and her final tragedy. According to the catalogue published by the Bibliothèque Nationale this play has been presented several times since 1916,[11] making it the most popular of Péguy's performed works. It was given at least in part during the summer festivals as late as 1975.

III   The Second Mystery

With his second mystery, *Le Porche du mystère de la deuxième vertu* (The Portico of the Mystery of the Second Virtue, pp. 527–670) published in 1911, Péguy left Joan behind. Although the poem is ostensibly recounted by the nun Madame Gervaise in free verse, actually Péguy does the talking. He speaks of his own children (pp. 541–2), mentions two thousand years with reference to the Bible and 1400 with reference to Joan (p. 623), and mingles the masculine gender with the feminine (p. 632). The work is a magnificent discourse, an entrance into a porch for the performance of the mystery of the second of the three virtues which is hope. Péguy characterizes faith as a wife, charity as a mother or older sister, and hope as a little girl (p. 536) who paradoxically leads the other two. He even pictures her as Cinderella (p. 644).

Hope as a child permits Péguy to refer to the hope that was born on Christmas Day early in the poem. He will return to Jesus in another context at the end of the work. Hope as a child symbolizes the young as the future hope of mankind just as Péguy's children symbolize his personal hope for the future. In speaking of his children Péguy returns to his preoccupation with absence for "He thinks with tenderness of the time when he will no longer be" (*Il pense avec tendresse à ce temps où il ne sera plus*, p. 546). The void of his absence will be filled by his children who like all children can even "weep in hope" (*ils pleurent en espérance*, p. 561). Hope sees, as Péguy puts it, what will be "in the future of eternity itself" (*dans le futur de l'éternité même*, p. 539).

Placing his children in the care of the Virgin gives Péguy the opportunity to dedicate a lovely hymn to the Mother of Heaven (pp. 567–9, 572–4). Hope as a child also suggests the three parables as told by St. Luke, those of the lost sheep, the lost drachma, and the lost child. Hope was born of the fear of loss in each parable and most particularly, of course, in the last. This paean to hope in its enormity becomes a veritable "abyss of hope" (*Abîme d'espérance*, p. 605) limited only by the patriotic refrain "France and Christianity must continue" (*il faut que France, il faut que chrétienté continue*, p. 558) that recurs with variations throughout the last hundred pages.

By way of conclusion Péguy offers what must be some of the most beautiful pages ever written on the subject of sleep and night. If "he who works, prays" (*celui qui travaille, prie*), "he who sleeps, [also] prays" (*Celui qui dort, prie*), for sleep is perhaps God's "most beautiful creation" (*plus belle création*), "the great secret of being indefatigable like a child" (*C'est le grand secret d'être infatigable comme un enfant*, p. 657). The dreamless sleep of the child takes place at night which leads Péguy to the night on Golgotha and the hope of the world that was born there. Péguy was no Shakespeare but in a language now grandiloquent, now homely, now formal, now familiar, he pours forth endless moving pages on hope in all its heavenly as well as terrestrial guises, making of the *Porche* along with *La Tapisserie de Notre Dame*, as a recent critic writes, "the most beautiful jewel in Péguy's poetic treasure."[12]

IV *The Third Mystery*

Péguy published his third mystery, *Le Mystère des saints innocents* (The Mystery of the Holy Innocents, pp. 671–823), in 1912 to celebrate the four hundred eighty-third anniversary of the deliverance of Orleans by Joan. Madame Gervaise and Joan are again on stage speaking in free verse printed in three type sizes, roman, italics, and heavy capitals. Péguy had already used this device which foretells in a modest way the typographical experiments of the surrealists and their successors. Péguy's point of departure is again the three virtues, faith, hope, and charity, but this time faith is a soldier, a church, and a tree, charity a doctor, a hospital, and a haven, while hope is the promise of the budding flower. Péguy again draws comparisons betwen night and day and again concludes that night is not the time for an anguished examination of conscience but for sleep (pp. 684–92).

One of his most striking images is that of the "immense fleet of prayers laden with the sins of the world" (*cette immense flotte de prières chargée des péchés du monde*, p. 699) that sails eternally towards God in triple formation. The Lord's Prayer leads the way, and is followed by "Hail Mary" and all the other prayers said in His honor. There is even a fourth fleet of all the unspoken prayers (p. 705). God created man free to seek his own salvation which brings Péguy to the story of St. Louis and the chronicler Joinville. The latter preferred to commit mortal sin rather than contract leprosy while St. Louis as a saint obviously preferred leprosy to sin (pp. 717–39). Péguy thus quotes Joinville at length and then Genesis (p. 743), and then the complete story of Joseph and his brothers (pp. 748–76). The point is that Joseph went into Egypt as did Jesus and St. Louis after him.

Occasionally the reader notes a particularly beautiful romantic line like *le couronnement du jugement et le commencement du Paradis et de ma Béatitude sera / Le coucher du soleil d'un éternel été* (the crowning of the judgment and the beginning of Paradise and of my Beatitude will be / The setting of the sun of an eternal summer, p. 745). The reader also encounters again the formula in an alexandrine, *Heureux celui qui resterait comme un enfant* (Happy he who would remain like a child, p. 785). Hope is a child, thus Péguy again quotes the Bible and Jesus when He said, "Suffer little children to come unto me" (p. 791), which leads Péguy to quote the story as told by St. Matthew and the Catholic Missal of the slaughter of the innocents by Herod. Because the innocent were children, they were the hope of the future. Because they were innocent, they entered directly into heaven. Because they were martyred in the place of and for Jesus, they made possible the hope of the world. They were borne away, as the Christian Latin poet Prudentius puts it, like nascent roses before the storm (p. 823).

Because Péguy reworks so many of his previous ideas in this third mystery, his inspiration seems to have dissipated somewhat. Because he quotes so often and at such length, his creative vigor appears to have weakened. No matter how much he hides behind the skirts of Joan and Madame Gervaise, Péguy seems in the end to have confused himself with God, and a rather garrulous God at that, a God strangely addicted to a uniquely French brand of patriotism. The third mystery does reveal again, however, that what at first glance seems to be a sprawling, formless mass, is actually a tightly controlled message with its various strands neatly woven into a story that is tragic but full of hope.

V   *Brief Interludes*

Although busy with the direction of the *Cahiers* and involved in the writing of more lengthy works, Péguy found time to publish nine short poems, six in 1912 and three in 1913, all in alexandrines. Péguy's sonnets almost always come in pairs, the masculine and the feminine he called them. Thus the first two of 1912, "L'Epave" (The Shipwreck) and "L'Urne" (The Urn), are variations on a theme. Using nautical terms the poet wonders in the former if we shall ever have, after pinning our fate on "A hope narrower than the Latin sail" (*Un espoir plus étroit que la voile latine*, p. 827), the courage to allow Jesus to direct the course of our life. In the latter he wonders if, "Frightened in the face of Latin anger" (*Epouvantés devant la colère latine*, p. 828), we shall dare to weep over "this humble earthen pot" (*cette humble terrine*) that was our life when "the grim reaper" (*le dur vendangeur*) calls us to judgment.

During the summer of 1912 Marcel Péguy translated Homer under the guidance of his father. Thus "The Blind Man" of the two sonnets "L'Aveugle" is the Greek poet. In the first Péguy notes that seven cities claim Homer but the only one to which he would give him is Athens, "The only one in which we are sure he was never seen" (*La seule où l'on soit sûr qu'on ne l'ait jamais vu,* p. 828). In the second sonnet two thousand years of experience have washed over the world and yet Homer is "The vagabond blind man [who] will always be the master, / Behind all that is said, of all that is not said" (*L'aveugle vagabond sera toujours le maître, / Sous tout ce qui se dit, de tout ce qui se tait,* p. 829). The inspiration for "Les Sept contre Thèbes" (Seven Against Thebes) was Aeschylus. The twenty quatrains are loaded with more than thirty-five exotic names of which the average reader might recognize eight or nine. The names of all the defenders and attackers of six of the gates of Thebes are listed. The most important gate is, of course, the seventh, the one at which "Etiocles was waiting for his brother Polynices" (*Etéocle attendait son frère Polynice,* p. 832) for their fatal fratricidal confrontation. Of the one hundred twenty "Chateaux of the Loire" (*Châteaux de Loire*) there is one that surpasses all others, "the souvenir that has left on these shores / A child who led her horse to the river" (*le souvenir qu'a laissé sur ces bords / Une enfant qui menait son cheval vers le fleuve,* p. 833), that is, Joan of Arc.

The two poems of "Les Sept contre Paris" (Seven Against Paris) belong to the same period but appeared in 1913. In the first, "Paris," seven sections of the city want to make something of Paris which she refuses to be. Instead, "the lady ate up her seven little sisters" (*la dame a mangé les sept petites soeurs,* p. 883) and brought them all together "Under the commandment of the towers of Notre Dame" (*Sous le commandement des tours de Notre-Dame*). "Paris" is a sonnet plus one line. The second poem, "La Banlieue" (The Suburbs), is composed of thirty quatrains plus two lines. Again lady Paris eats up the seven suburbs and more while assimilating unto herself a whole series of famous people of the eighteenth and nineteenth centuries, all inventions, ideas, and things, and she does it "Under the commandment of the towers of Notre Dame" (*Sous le commandement des tours de Notre-Dame,* p. 887). Péguy's son has quite rightly called these poems "perhaps the last of the Parnassian school" (p. 18). Although the rhyme scheme varies, they are balanced in form, cool and "classical" in content, descriptive in technique, and while they have nothing much to say, they say it in a charming way.

The last short poem, "Sainte Geneviève patronne de Paris" (St. Genevieve, Patron Saint of Paris, pp. 925–32) of 1913, is composed of a quatrain, fifteen stanzas of ten lines, plus six quatrains. Péguy addresses himself to the shepherdess of Nanterre so that each ten line stanza begins, "You who know her ..." (*Vous qui la connaissez ...*), meaning, of course, Paris. All stanzas but the last six end with a variation of the formula, "The vagabond city and nevertheless sedentary" (*La ville vagabonde et pourtant sédentaire,* p. 927). The ten line stanzas rhyme abbaabbacd and while a and b may change, c and d remain the same through all fifteen stanzas. St. Geneviève has obviously known Paris in her many moods, her triumphs and tragedies, her victories and defeats and she will be the one to speak to God in behalf of the city "when the last swallow has flown away" (*quand aura volé la dernière hirondelle,* p. 931). This is another "Parnassian" poem that is a paean to Paris.

VI   *The First Tapestry*

Péguy published his first tapestry, *La Tapisserie de sainte Geneviève et de Jeanne d'Arc* (*The Tapistry of St. Genevieve and Joan of Arc,* pp. 835–80), in 1912. Dedicated to Geneviève Favre, Péguy's friend and patroness and the mother of the Catholic philosopher Jacques Maritain, the tapestry weaves together the stories of the two shepherdesses, the patron saint of Paris and the savior of France. The tapestry is composed of nine poems, four of which are sonnets. It also includes a sonnet plus one line, a sonnet plus a tercet, a poem of five quatrains, a sonnet plus three hundred eighteen tercets plus one line, and a poem of twenty-nine quatrains plus two tercets. The first poem commemorates the fourteen hundred first anniversary of the death

of St. Geneviève. The fourth poem celebrates the five hundred
first anniversary of the birth of Joan of Arc. The first three
poems recount quite simply how the shepherdess from Nanterre,
St. Geneviève, came to guard a quite different flock, that of
"this monster of stone" (*ce monstre de pierre*, p. 839), "this
enormous inn" (*cette auberge énorme*, p. 840), that is Paris.
The fourth, fifth, and sixth poems tell of St. Geneviève's
pleasure upon seeing after nine hundred twenty years the
arrival of "The greatest beauty of all her lineage" (*La plus grande
beauté de tout son parentage*, p. 842), "The holiest girl after
the Holy Virgin" (*La fille la plus sainte après la Sainte Vierge*,
p. 843), "The girl from Lorraine like no other" (*La fille de
Lorraine à nulle autre pareille*, p. 844), Joan of Arc. She comes
forth when the kingdom is in shambles and the city is rent with
civil discord. She arrives with her standard bearing the arms
of Jesus.

In the eighth poem Péguy pits the arms of Jesus against
those of Satan and spends three hundred sixteen tercets develop-
ing the contrasts and differences. At first the reader is overwhelmed by this seemingly endless flow of attributes, but
eventually the repetition of phrases and especially of rhymes
becomes vaguely annoying and faintly embarrassing. It also becomes somewhat amusing. I rather like "the nail in the boot"
(*le clou dans la botte*, p. 850), "the impudent look" (*le regard
impudent*, p. 856), and "elbows on the table" (*Les coudes sur
la table*, p. 861) as the work of the devil. In the same homely
vein St. Peter is described in his bark as "the old fisher of man
seated on his behind, / Depopulating the Ocean, the lake, and
the river" (*le vieux pêcheur d'homme assis sur son derrière, /
Dépeuplant l'Océan, le lac et la rivière*, p. 855), obviously in
the service of Jesus. Women's liberation would probably not be
pleased to find "Desire and woman" (*Le désir et la femme*, p.
851) ascribed to the devil any more than liberals would be to
find "The vote, the mandate, and suffrage" (*Le vote, le mandat
et la suffragerie*, p. 860) given to him. It is a shame to see
"bitter pumpkin" (*Cette citrouille amère*, p. 852) denigrated.
Unfortunately, the French with their culinary expertise, have
never really conquered the art of the pumpkin pie. Péguy can
draw effective contrasts like "the ephemeral imprint / Of our

footsteps in the sand" (*l'éphémère empreinte / De nos pas sur le sable*) with "the eternal imprint / Of His footsteps in the sand" (*l'éternelle empreinte / De ses pas sur le sable,* p. 853). It is confusing, however, that "prose" (*la prose,* p. 857) should be on the right side while "literature" (*la littérature,* p. 866) is on the wrong side. Péguy's poetry is certainly not prose, but is it then "only" literature? Péguy became acquainted with Verlaine's religious sonnets in *Sagesse* in 1911. Perhaps he also noted the symbolist poet's famous pejorative line, "And all the rest is literature."

From the very first tercet dedicated to Satan, Péguy again reveals his anti-intellectualism by including in it "The knowledge of the knowledgeable" or perhaps better "The intellectuality of the intellectuals" (*Le savoir des savants,* p. 849). He goes on to include "scientificism" (*le scientificisme*) and "the laboratory" (*le laboratoire,* p. 850), "the philologist and his hardware" (*le philologue et sa quincaillerie*) and of course "the theorem" (*le théorème,* p. 859) and "psychiatry" (*psychiatrie,* p. 864). Many of the noun endings are pejorative as in "the Aristotelian" (*l'aristotélique*) who is indeed at his worst "when he explains" (*Et le pire de tout c'est bien quand il explique,* p. 863). Plagued as Péguy and his family were by illness, the reader is surprised to see him take a swipe, reminiscent of Molière's at doctors in general when he writes of "the bad doctor, / (But are there any good ones?)" (*le mauvais docteur, / (Mais en est-il de bons?),* p. 865). Near the conclusion Péguy returns to his theme of "a just war" (*une juste guerre,* p. 873), which he claims, somewhat dubiously, as an attribute of Jesus. The mention of war does, however, bring Péguy back to his original subject in the last ten tercets. St. Geneviève again sees Joan arriving with her cohort under the standard of Jesus, she who was "The greatest saint after St. Mary" (*La sainte la plus grande après sainte Marie,* p. 875).

Just as Péguy wrote three hundred twenty tercets to conclude the two quatrains of his eighth "sonnet," so he wrote twenty-nine quatrains to introduce the two tercets of his last poem, using only the rhymes *-age* and *-gnons.* In them he recounts all the horrors, spiritual as well as physical, St. Geneviève witnessed before Joan finally appeared on the horizon, "the most beautiful child of her long lineage" (*la plus belle enfant de ses longs patronages*, p. 880). The nine "sonnets" are pleasant enough and do link St. Geneviève and Joan of Arc in an unusual and unexpected way. But somehow the calculation of all those rhymes, the enormity of detail after detail, do not build vertically as they must in such poetry. They are strung along horizontally like the beads of a rosary. They do make a circle but along the way all human passion, all psychological insight is reduced to a litany that has somehow lost its meaning, its relevance, and its power to move the reader.

CHAPTER 7

The Poet: 1913

THE second tapestry, *La Tapisserie de Notre Dame* (*The Tapestry of Our Lady*)[1] published in 1913, is dedicated to Péguy's friend Joseph Lotte. Its ten poems bring together the cathedrals of Paris and Chartres, more particularly Our Lady of both. For reasons we shall see later, Péguy did not publish the tenth poem along with the rest of the tapestry. Only four of the six poems comprising a total of nineteen stanzas are dedicated to Paris. The remaining two hundred fifteen stanzas are addressed to Chartres. The great difference is explained by the two pilgrimages Péguy made on foot from Paris to Chartres June 14–17, 1912, and July 25-28, 1913. The fifth poem contains some of Péguy's most frequently anthologized stanzas.

The central image of the first four poems is based on the ambiguity of the expression *la lourde nef* (p. 893) which can mean both "the heavy nave" of a cathedral and "the heavy hull" of a ship. Thus in the first poem, "Présentation de Paris à Notre Dame" (Presentation of Paris to Our Lady, pp. 893-4), Paris is a galley whose rowers are about to take on cargo. The contrast is between the light load of "our poor virtues" (*nos pauvres vertus*) and the "weight of our sins paid for by [Her] son" (*Du poids de nos péchés payés par votre fils*). In the second poem, a sonnet entitled "Paris vaisseu de charge" (Paris Cargo Ship, p. 894), Paris becomes a double cargo ship symbolized by the two banks of the Seine, the two types of cargo symbolized by gold and grain, by the physical and the spiritual. The painful history of Paris is so full of "a so severe regret" (*un regret si sévère*) "That the chief will take it for a sack of prayer" (*Que le chef le prendra pour un sac de prière*) and raise it high above this "Double cargo ship at the feet of Notre Dame" (*Double vaisseau de charge aux pieds de Notre Dame*).

104

The third poem, also a sonnet, is called "Paris double galère" (Paris Double Galley, pp. 894-5). A city of "private sorrows and public virtues" (*les deuils privés et les vertus publiques*), Paris has survived kingdoms and republics and although its inhabitants are "Forced laborers sons of forced laborers" (*Forçats fils de forçats*), they will row with all their might, these "Galley slaves bedded down at the feet of Notre Dame" (*Galériens couchés aux pieds de Notre Dame*). The final sonnet is "Paris vaisseau de guerre" (Paris Ship of War, p. 895). The fathers of today's Parisians "have flowered [her] with the blood of the most beautiful death" (*Ils t'ont fleuri du sang de la plus belle mort*) in defense of freedom, fatherland, and religion. Thus the present-day inhabitants are such "Soldiers sons of soldiers" (*Soldats fils de soldats*) that they will be made "valets of [Her] gaping canons, / Green monsters crouching at the feet of Notre Dame" (*valets de tes canons béants, / Monstres verts accroupis aux pieds de Notre Dame*).

The opening line of the fifth poem echoes that of the first but Péguy has left Paris on foot for Chartres on a pilgrimage to thank the Virgin for curing his sick son. The "Présentation de la Beauce à Notre Dame de Chartres" (Presentation of the Beauce to Our Lady of Chartres, pp. 896–907) describes in eighty-nine quatrains of alexandrines rhyming abba his trip across the Beauce, the great plain south and east of Paris that is the breadbasket of France and in the middle of which rises the glorious cathedral. The splendid opening quatrains set the tone:

> Etoile de la mer voici la lourde nappe
> Et la profonde houle et l'océan des blés
> Et la mouvante écume et nos greniers comblés,
> Votre regard sur cette immense chape
>
> Et voici votre voix sur cette lourde plaine
> Et nos amis absents et nos coeurs dépeuplés,
> Voici le long de nous nos poings désassemblés,
> Et notre lassitude et notre force pleine.   (p. 896)
>
> Star of the sea here is the heavy cloth
> And the profound swell and the ocean of grain
> And the moving foam and our full graneries,
> Your glance over this immense cope

And here is your voice over this heavy plain
And our absent friends and our depopulated hearts,
Here are our fists relaxed at our side
And our lassitude and our full strength.

Several details are to be noted. For a man who never sailed the sea Péguy uses an amazing number of nautical images. The theme of absence, expressed as early as his first work, also reappears. Yet, while spiritual absence is implicit and explicit in much of his poetry, solitude becomes personal here for the first time. Friends may be absent simply geographically or through death and a heart may be emptied of thoughts of others in order to be filled with the message of divine love. But somehow a heart that has been depopulated sounds more desolate and more desperate than that. In the two stanzas Péguy moves from the endless fields of grain to himself across Her look that seeks him out and Her voice that calls to him. The vast panorama described in rolling alexandrines is reduced to the humble details of a lonely, empty heart, a relaxed fist, and to lassitude. At the last moment lassitude is contrasted with the full force of his faith that will enable him to complete his mission. The breadth of this vision is pitted against the abruptness of the rhymes in *-appe* and *-blés* and *-plés* only to be enlarged both phonetically and figuratively by the rhyme *plaine-pleine*. In the third stanza the rhyme becomes *reine-peine*, linking again the Virgin with the miserable sinner.

Unfortunately, the poem goes on for eighty-seven more stanzas. In the last eighteen Péguy states that he has come to pray for a boy, not his son, who died a stupid and useless death. The boy was probably René Bichet who died of an accidental overdose of drugs at the age of twenty-six. After the careful enumeration of all the people encountered and the places visited, the first view of the cathedral and the inspiration received from it, the conclusion of the poem is like a last sigh:

Nous ne demandons rien, refuge du pécheur,
Que la dernière place en votre Purgatoire,
Pour pleurer longuement notre tragique histoire,
Et contempler de loin votre jeune splendeur.   (p. 907)

> We ask nothing more, refuge of the sinner,
> Than the last place in your Purgatory,
> In order to weep at length over our tragic story,
> And contemplate from afar your young splendor.

Is "our tragic story" that of the dead youth and Péguy or simply that of Péguy, or is it the tragic story of all mankind? The ambiguity of "our" moves the poem from the specific to the general so that we have all participated in the pilgrimage and benefitted spiritually from the physical experience. That is, if the reader has not fallen by the wayside before he reaches Chartres.

While at Chartres Péguy composed five poem-prayers in the cathedral. The first, "Prière de résidence" (Prayer of Residence, pp. 908-16) with its sixty-two quatrains, is almost as long as the "Presentation of the Beauce." Ten of the stanzas begin with "Here is..." (*Voici...*) and forty with "That which everywhere else..." (*Ce qui partout ailleurs...*). The contrasts between what exists elsewhere and its opposite in the cathedral are frequently finely drawn, interesting, and moving. Poetic and almost romantic is the couplet, "That which everywhere else is a putting on of airs / Is here only a rose and footsteps in the sand" (*Ce qui partout ailleurs est un rengorgement / N'est ici qu'une rose et des pas sur le sable*, p. 915). The conclusion is again a resigned but hopeful sigh:

> Ce qui partout ailleurs est la route suivie
> N'est ici qu'un paisible et fort détachement,
> Et dans un calme temple et loin d'un plat tourment
> L'attente d'une mort plus vivante que vie.

> That which elsewhere is the travelled road
> Is here only a peaceful and strong detachment,
> And in a calm temple and far from a flat torment
> The waiting for a death more alive than life.

The second prayer is a "Prière de demande" (Prayer of Intercession, pp. 916-7) in twelve quatrains, ten of which begin, "We do not ask..." (*Nous ne demandons pas...*). Péguy would not ask for the impossible, only that we be able "to maintain under [Her] commandments / A fidelity stronger than death" (*garder sous vos commandements / Une fidélité plus forte que la mort*). The third "Prière de confidence" (Prayer of Trust, pp. 917–8) has only eight quatrains but does include Péguy's third use of the rhyme *nappe-chape*. Péguy has so much confidence in the Virgin that he knows whatever he achieves will be "not at all by virtue for we have almost none, / And not at all through duty for we do not like it" (*non point par vertu car nous n'en avons guère, / Et non point par devoir car nous ne l'aimons pas*). Péguy's masochism has become so pronounced that he speaks of "this dumb need to be more unhappy" (*ce besoin sourd d'être plus malheureux*) in order "at least to hold on to honor, / And keep for it alone our poor tenderness" (*au moins pour tenir l'honneur, / Et lui garder lui seul notre pauvre tendresse*). Despite Péguy, it seems that one need not necessarily be unhappy in order to hold on to his honor. The fourth "Prière de report" (Prayer of Audit, pp. 919–22) is composed of twenty-three stanzas, seventeen of which begin with variations of "We have..." (*Nous avons...*) and four with "If it is permitted..." (*S'il est permis...*). Since we have known only Our Lady's graces of war, mourning, pain, joy, and misery, "We ask for nothing" (*Nous ne demandons rien,* p. 921). One critic maintains that "With the 'Prayers in the Cathedral,' Péguy achieves the miracle of bringing about the perfect fusion between poetry and the mystical experience, of expressing through human language, an ineffable reality." This critic then calls the poems, "Marvelous 'night music,' " and states that they "represent in the career of the poet a summit which he had never attained and which he will never again surpass."[2] Contrary to this praise, the four prayers seem to me to be among Péguy's most mournful and least successful works, weighed down as they are by their excessive length, monotonous repetitions, and dolorous tone.

Péguy probably did not publish the fifth "Prière de déférence" (Prayer of Bestowal, pp. 922–4) because its twenty-one stanzas begin, as did the "Presentation of the Beauce," with a very personal revelation. By this time Péguy had alienated so many friends that the opening line, "So many friends turned away from this solitary heart" (*Tant d'amis détournés de ce coeur solitaire*) would have been a painful admission in public, even if he did qualify it with the second line, "Have not at all worn out love or fidelity" (*N'ont point lassé l'amour ni la fidélité*). Out of deference to Our Lady no one can enter Her sanctuary who does "not consent and allow and maintain and wish, / From the thickness of a world to be loved less than [She]" (*ne consente et laisse et ne prétend et veuille, / De l'épaisseur d'un monde être aimé moins que vous*). Or Péguy may not have wanted to publish this poem because he felt it was not worthy of the others. Of the ten poems, only the "Presentation of the Beauce" occasionally approaches great poetry and then its near greatness is drowned in its own enormity. As one critic puts it, "when, after having read these poems, one thinks suddenly of Baudelaire, a gap opens up and Péguy recedes."[3]

I The First Woman

Late in 1913 Péguy published his last poetic work, *Eve* (pp. 933–1174), a monstrous poem of one thousand nine hundred eleven quatrains, that is, seven thousand six hundred forty-four lines all of which are alexandrines except for the final hemistich. The poem must be among the longest ever written in French and suffers from its immensity. The rhyme scheme alternates abba abab in no discernible pattern. Jesus is ostensibly the speaker although Péguy forgets himself and has Jesus speaking of Jesus as only the poet could. In order to discuss the poem I have divided it arbitrarily into nine sections:
1. You have not yet known... (*Vous n'avez plus connu...*, stanzas 1–146, pp. 935–53):
Jesus speaks to Eve pointing out all the things in this world she could not have known as the first woman. She could not have known God's grace and all that came with it, the animals, the plants, the inventions, the seasons. The world was a vast garden in which man was respected by the beasts and thus became their natural shepherd. Péguy returns to the idea of shepherds, or rather shepherdesses, in the conclusion of his poem. In a development within this section beginning "And God Himself..." (*Et Dieu lui-Même...*, stanzas 32–68, pp. 939–43), God considers His creation and calls it good. If Eve did not

know all the good, she also did not know all the evil that came into the world with the race she begot.

2. Oh woman, you who organize ...(*O femme qui rangez* ..., stanzas 147–517, pp. 953–99):

Eve as the first woman provides Péguy with the opportunity to expatiate at great length on all the work woman does in organizing a world disorganized by man. While praising woman Péguy in his enthusiasm slips into a sort of anti-feminism. Although Eve, Mary, Geneviève, and Joan are his guiding lights, most women including his wife seem to receive short shrift. He could be humorous on the subject, however. Witness the quatrain that begins "Women, I tell you, you would organize even God, / If He descended one day into your house" (*Femmes, je vous le dis, vous rangeriez Dieu même, / S'il descendait un jour dedans votre maison*, p. 954). But Péguy is not often so amusing: "Oh women, you who can in the cruelest game / Cheat with a tranquil heart and a light hand" (*O femmes qui pouvez dans le plus cruel jeu / Tricher d'un coeur tranquille et d'une main légère*, p. 764). But woman washes, sweeps, cleans, and watches, classifies, sees, gathers, and knows. Although Péguy maintains she frequently does so when it is too late, nevertheless "man is only an idiot before your broom" (*l'homme n'est qu'un sot devant votre balai*, p. 974). In a very long development beginning "And when ... " (*Et quand* ..., stanzas 327–411, pp. 976–86), Péguy asks if, when all is over and done, she will have the strength to lead her mourning flock back to the way. Peguy's pessimism also comes to the fore in stanzas like:

> Et par là vous savez combien l'homme exagère
> Quand il dit qu'il déteste et quand il dit qu'il aime.
> Et qu'il n'est point de lieu sur la terre étrangère
> Ni pour un grand amour ni pour un grand blasphème.
>
> (p. 989)

> And thereby you know how much man exaggerates
> When he says he detests and when he says he loves.
> And that there is no room at all on this alien earth
> For a great love or for a great blasphemy.

3. One did not nourish ... (*On ne nourrissait pas* ..., stanzas 517–30, pp. 999–1001):

In this relatively brief development Péguy enumerates all the things of this world that man did not encourage, the bad and the good, only to end up with "solutions worse than the problem" (*solutions pire que le problème*, p. 1001).

4. And I, I salute you... (*Et moi je vous salue*..., stanzas 531–742, pp. 1001–28):

Péguy salutes Eve for all she did for the human race although she is remembered as the "queen of disgrace" (*reine de disgrâce*, p. 1001). The section includes several shorter developments including "You have put so much..." (*Vous en avez tant mis*..., stanzas 538–47, pp. 1002–3) in which Péguy recognizes all she gave the world. Opposed to "The others [who] have known only..." (*Les autres [qui] n'ont connu que*... stanzas 555–65), pp. 1004–5) the wickedness and tragedies of the world, "You alone know..." (*Seule vous le savez*..., stanzas 566–742, pp. 1006–28) that all we do and have today is not the equal of "the good old days" which were for Péguy any time before 1880. Only rarely does the reader encounter an enigmatic and haunting quatrain that gives pause for thought:

> Les autres n'ont connu que la commune honte.
> Mais vous avez connu cette ruelle oblique
> Qui descend sur la foire et la place publique
> Et d'où nul ne revient et que nul ne remonte.   (p. 1013)

> Others have known only the common shame.
> But you have known this oblique little street
> That descends to the fair and the public square.
> And from which no one returns and that no one mounts again.

Péguy's lack of faith in mankind frequently intrudes:

> Seule vous le savez, nos plus beaux sentiments
> Ne durent jamais plus que l'espace d'un jour.
> Et l'amour le plus ferme et le plus dur amour
> Ne dure jamais plus de quelques moments.   (p. 1020)

> You alone know that our most beautiful sentiments
> Never last more than the space of a day.
> And the firmest love and the soundest love
> Never lasts more than a few moments.

Nor can I agree with Péguy's views on the "supernatural good" of poverty:

> Seule vous le savez, nos réclamations
> Ne réclament jamais que des biens temporels.
> Nous ne réclamons pas ces biens surnaturels,
> De pauvreté, de peine et de privations.   (p. 1024)

> You alone know that our complaints
> Never beg except for temporal goods.
> We do not beg for those supernatural goods,
> Of poverty, pain, and privations.

Which brings us to Péguy's most often quoted lines.
5. Happy those who died... (*Heureux ceux qui sont morts*..., stanzas 743–62, pp. 1028–30):

These twenty stanzas must be among the most beautiful poetically, on the subject of patriotic death in French literature. Béranger had already used the formula in one of his *Chansons* of 1823, "Le Vieux Sergent": "Happy he who died in these fetes" (*Heureux celui qui mourut dans ces fêtes*) which Péguy quoted in his essay "A nos amis, à nos abonnés" of 1909.[4] Péguy could also have found it in Hugo's *Odes et ballades*: "Happy he who, far from the path of a servile crowd" (*Heureux qui, loin des pas d'une foule asservie*) and "Happy he who can, in the bosom of a solitary valley" (*Heureux qui peut, au sein du vallon solitaire*). The great rolling alexandrines express in a noble and majestic cadence the return of mortal man to the earth from which he came, the final return to God. They have become a "part of the national heritage"[5] of the French yet I cannot agree with Péguy's major premise:

> Heureux ceux qui sont morts pour la terre charnelle,
> Mais pourvu que ce fût dans une juste guerre.
> Heureux ceux qui sont morts pour quatre coins de terre.
> Heureux ceux qui sont morts d'une mort solennelle.   (p. 1028)

> Happy those who died for this carnal earth,
> But provided that it was in a just war.
> Happy are those who died for four corners of earth.
> Happy are those who died a solemn death.

I am not convinced that a single person of the eight million casualties of World War I, except perhaps for Péguy, was really happy to have died, no matter how just the war. What is being said spoils for me the beauty of how it is being said. Nevertheless, if they really had to die, I find myself agreeing with Péguy's last stanza:

> Que Dieu mette avec eux dans le juste plateau
> Ce qu'ils ont tant aimé, quelques grammes de terre.
> Un peu de cette vigne, un peu de ce coteau,
> Un peu de ce ravin sauvage et solitaire.   (p. 1030)

> May God place with them on the scales of justice
> That which they loved so much, a few grams of earth.
> A little of this vine, a little of this hillside.
> A little of this savage and solitary ravine.

But even Péguy's wish for "Peace to the men of war" (*Paix aux hommes de guerre*, p. 1030) does not allay my suspicions of his sentiments.

6.   Mother, here are your sons . . . (*Mère voici vos fils . . .* , stanzas 763–1005, pp. 1030–60):

The soldiers are, of course, the sons of Eve who have given their lives and deserve to be shown God's mercy. The blood they have spilled is the blood Jesus spilled who, like them, is a mortal man. But just as every man is body and soul, mortal and immortal, so the infant Jesus was born of mortal woman but is immortal. As He raises His enormous eyes He sees all the pairs of animals and men, like the parade to Noah's ark, that come to worship Him in His double heritage. The section concludes with a long development in which Péguy asks, "Have we . . . " (*Avons-nous . . .* , stanzas 969–1005, pp. 1056–60) abandoned the infant Jesus through our lack of faith. Thus the child slept . . . (*Ainsi l'enfant dormait . . .* , stanzas 1006–76, pp. 1061–9):

Jesus slept and while doing so He brought the Christian world into being. He slept "As Moses slept . . . " (*Comme dormait Moïse . . .* , stanzas 1042–70, pp. 1065–9) but no king's daughter comes to save Him. As Moses slept in the land of Memphis, so Jesus slept in the land of Israel but "He was going to attempt the enormous exception, / The long resurrection of man enterred" (*Il allait essayer l'énorme exception,* / *Le long resurge-ment de l'homme enseveli,* p. 1069).

7. He was going to inherit... (*Il allait hériter...,* stanzas 1077–1299, pp. 1069–97):

In so doing Jesus was going to inherit all the history of the Western World up to His time. In that sense it can be said He inherited from Alexander, Herodotus, Hercules, Theseus, and Darius (pp. 1084–5), as well as Agamemnon, Plato, Aristotle, and Zeno (p. 1086). His coming was to put an end to the influence of the East:

> Il allait hériter du monde occidental
> Des cheveux des varechs et des verts goémons.
> Il allait aveugler par ces nouveaux limons
> Les infiltrations du monde oriental.   (p. 1071)

> He was going to inherit from the occidental world,
> The hair of the brown seaweed and of the green.
> He was going to blind with these new muds
> The infiltrations of the oriental world.

He was going to inherit the good and bad of all times.

8. And it is not... (*Et ce n'est pas...,* stanzas 1300–1778, pp. 1097–1157):

Actually this section is composed of two parts, one in the present tense (stanzas 1300–1396, pp. 1097–1122), and one in the future tense "And it will not be..." (*Et ce ne sera pas...,* stanzas 1397–1778, pp. 1122–57). The tense does not make much difference because Péguy is simply listing all those things we do not need and shall not need on judgment day, including geography, typography, archeology, philology, sociology, bibliographies, libraries, catalogues, anthropologists, psychologists, conservatories, professors of history, and seismographs (pp. 1097–9), to name a few. He enumerate all the advances, intellectual as well as material, that constitute "modern" Western civilization and in so doing reveals again his own brand of anti-intellectualism.

9. One died... (*L'une est morte...,* stanzas 1779–1911, pp. 1157–74):

The French will not need all these things because they have

chosen two ancient and unique shepherdesses, St. Geneviève
and Joan of Arc, to lead them. On this patriotic note Péguy concludes:

> L'une est morte ainsi d'une mort solennelle
> Sur ses quatre-vingt-dix ou quatre-vingt-douze ans
> Et les durs villageois et les durs paysans,
> La regardant vieillir l'avaient crue éternelle.
>
> Et l'autre est morte ainsi d'une mort solennelle.
> Elle n'avait passé ses humbles diz-neuf ans
> Que de quatre ou cinq mois et sa cendre charnelle
>   Fut dispersée aux vents.   (p. 1174)

> Thus one died a solemn death
> In her ninetieth or ninety-second year
> And the hardened villagers and the hardened peasants
> Watching her grow old believed her to be eternal.
>
> Thus the other died a solemn death.
> She had passed her humble nineteenth year
> By only four or five months and her earthly ashes
>   Were scattered to the winds.

Thus *Eve* is another impressive statement of faith if not quite
"the most considerable work produced in Catholicism since the
fourteenth century" as Péguy himself claimed (p. 1520), and no
matter how one chooses to translate "considerable." Most of the
quatrains are humdrum with only occasionally a spark of true
poetry. The endless lists never build to create something new
like those of Rabelais and Hugo, as Butor has demonstrated.[6] The
countless repetitions numb the reader's sensitivities until he can
no longer follow Péguy's developments. Most readers would
be daunted by one thousand nine hundred eleven quatrains
before getting started. And most would give up before finishing
ten pages. Péguy, who would not bow to the necessities of life or
literature, defeated himself and his reader at the same time. I
leave to the reader the experience of analyzing the eight hundred
eighty-three quatrains of *Eve* (pp. 1389–1489) published posthumously in 1939.

II *The First Ballades*

After Péguy's death several manuscripts were discovered including a variant of the first act of *Jeanne d'Arc* (pp. 1181–98), two sections of the *Mystère de la charité de Jeanne d'Arc* that Péguy himself eliminated and that were published in 1926 and 1956 (pp. 1199–1262), a series of one thousand one hundred nine *Quatrains* sub-titled *Premier Livre des ballades* (*First Book of Ballades*, pp. 1263–1388), the quatrains from *Eve* noted above, and *La Ballade du coeur* (*The Ballade of the Heart*),[7] among other shorter works. The student of Péguy will want to consult these works for their historical importance and for what they reveal about Péguy's literary development.

The *Quatrains*, probably written in 1911 and 1912, show us a side of Péguy not often revealed in his other poetic works. Each quatrain is composed of two couplets of a hemistich and a line of four syllables rhyming mostly abab, rarely abba, once or twice abac abac, and even not at all. Péguy intended to organize them but we must accept them in the order in which they were found or follow the attempts of others to create an order not indicated by Péguy.

Many of the subjects near to Péguy are treated again at great length, the four cardinal virtues and the three theological virtues, St. Mary, the cathedrals of France. Historical allusions include Charlemagne, Napoleon, King David, Caesar, Cheops, Charles X, and Louis-Philippe. Literary allusions extend from Corneille to Lamartine, Hugo, and Dumas *fils*. Péguy probably knew by heart more of Hugo than any of his contemporaries or succesors and among the classics Corneille and his *Polyeucte* were his heroes. He wrote about both Hugo and Corneille at length in his essays, as we shall see.

Only once in his poetic works have I noted that Péguy makes unflattering references to his pet peeves and that was the allusion in "Les Sept contre Paris" to "Renan and the Rigid Taine" (*Renan et rigide Taine*, p. 885), the two fomentors of "modern" France. In the quatrains Péguy calls the literary historian, Gustave Lanson, the Duke of Sorbonne (p. 1330) while he devotes no less than nine quatrains to Ernest Lavisse, director of the École Normale Supérieure, under the name of *Le Nouvion de Thiérache* because Lavisse owns a counry home in a village of that name (pp. 1368–9). But these barbs are nothing compared to Péguy's diatribes in prose against the two men and many others, as we have seen.

The surprising aspect of the quatrains is what they reveal about Péguy's private and emotional life, a subject hardly approached in any of his poetic works. Although the allusions are veiled and discreet, they are all the more moving for that. A few quotations will suffice:

O coeur inexploré,
  Vaste univers,
Idole dédorée,
  Jardin d'hiver.   (p. 1271)

Oh unexplored heart,
  Vast universe,
Tarnished idol,
  Winter garden.

Prisonnier d'un secret
  Plus grand que toi,
Tu gardes ta prison,
  O coeur jaloux.   (p. 1279)

Prisoner of a secret
  Greater than you,
You keep to your prison,
  Oh jealous heart.

Tu n'oubliéras jamais,
  Coeur obsédé,
Un bonheur désormais
  Impossédé.   (p. 1382)

You will never forget,
  Obsessed heart,
A happiness forever more
  Unpossessed.

Aside from these revelations the quatrains are best left to the student of Péguy and his rhymes.

CHAPTER 8

The Theme of Absence

THE one theme that most of Péguy's poetic works share is absence. Péguy looks at absence from many points of view and in so doing reveals unexpected aspects of this rather commonplace and frequently overworked concept. His analysis certainly far transcends the simple nostalgia of homesickness. He considers "absence to" as well as "absence from," the presence that is absence and the absence that is presence, psychological absence in addition to physical absence, temporary absence and eternal absence, one's own absence and that of others, a future absence and a present absence that is death and the presence that is suffering.

The Christian or religious and perhaps even metaphysical basis for the theme is given in a prose work, the essay "Toujours de la grippe" of 1900. In this imaginary dialogue with a doctor who is Péguy saying to himself "Physician, heal thyself," the sick man, who is also the non-believer Péguy, says:

—Note, doctor, for it is time to say it, that these Christians whom I reproach for having loved or for having received sickness and human death admitted also, admitted above all that there was an eternal suffering, and an eternal sickness, and eternal contemporaneous death, or, in order to speak exactly co-eternal with all their happiness, with their eternal life, with their beatitude, and their health
—That, my friend, is an article of their faith.
—I shall attack their Christian faith then. What is most foreign to us in it, and I shall say the word, that which is barbarous, that to which we shall never consent, that which haunts the best Christians, the reason why the best Christians have slipped away, or silently turned away, my master, is this: that strange combination of life and death that we call damnation, that strange reinforcement of presence through absence and the reinforcement of all through eternity.[1]

118

The real sickness of the Christian faith is thus eternal damnation. According to that doctrine, we are simultaneously dead and alive. We are absent because we are dead, but we are present through our suffering, the suffering that harried and harassed us throughout our life as it will throughout our death, and through eternity. It is indeed a "strange reinforcement of presence through absence" since we are condemned to be present though absent.

Péguy had already used a variation of this theme of the "reinforcement of presence through absence" in his triptych *Jeanne d'Arc* of 1897. Near the end of the first play, *A Domremy,* Joan says good-bye to family and home in the name of the Meuse River and in so doing speaks of another kind of absence:

> O Meuse inépuisable et douce à mon enfance,
> Qui passes dans les prés auprès de la maison,
> C'est en ce moment-ci que je m'en vais en France:
> O ma Meuse, à présent je m'en vais pour de bon.
>
> O maison de mon père où je filais la laine,
> Maison de pierre forte, ô ma douce maison,
> Je m'en vais pour de bon dans la bataille humaine,
>
> O voici que je vais m'en aller pour de bon.
>
> Pourtant je ne sens pas l'émoi de la partance
> Et ne viens pas vous faire à présent mes adieux:
> C'est que violà huit mois que mon âme est en France,
> Violà huit mois déjà qu'elle est où je la veux.
>
> Mon âme est en allée en la ville du siège,
> Avec les défenseurs qui s'acharnent là-bas.
> Mes pas vont s'éloigner tout à l'heure en la neige,
> Mais mon âme a passé dans le pays là-bas.
>
> Vous tous, que j'aimais tant quand j'étais avec vous,
> O vous que j'aimai tant quand je m'en fus en France,
> A présent je vous aime encor plus, loin de vous:
> Mon âme a commencé l'étrange amour d'absence.
>
> A présent loin de vous, je vous aime encor plus
> Qu'au temps de la partance ou de la demeurance;

O j'aime étrangement la demeure où je fus,
A présent que mon âme a sa demeure en France.

Et j'aime étrangement ceux que j'aimais déjà,
Car je sens comme on aime alors qu'on est fidèle;
Mon âme sait aimer ceux qui ne sont pas là;
Mon âme sait aimer ceux qui restent loin d'elle.[2]

Oh Meuse inexhaustible and sweet in my childhood,
That passes through the fields near my house,
It is at this moment that I am going away to France:

Oh my Meuse, I am now going away for good.

Oh house of my father where I spun the wool,
Strong house of stone, oh my sweet home,
I am going away for good in the human battle,
Oh now I am going to go away for good.

Nevertheless I do not feel the emotion of departure
And I do not come now to say my good-byes:
My soul has been in France for eight months.
It has been where I want it to be for eight months already.

My soul has gone to the city under siege,
With the defenders who are persisting down there.
My footsteps are soon going to go off through the snow,
But my soul has gone over to the country down there.

All of you, whom I loved so much when I was with you,
Oh you whom I loved so much when I was away in France,
Now I love you even more, far from you:
My soul has begun the strange love of absence.

At present far from you, I love you even more
Than at the time of departure or of staying,
Oh I love strangely the place where I was,
Now that my soul has its abode in France.

And I love strangely those whom I loved already,
For I feel as one loves when one is faithful;
My soul knows how to love those who are not there;
My soul knows how to love those who remain far away.

Joan expresses here that "strange love of absence" according to which, although she is still physically in Lorraine, she is spiritually in Orleans and has been for eight months. Although the actual moment of departure is at hand, her heart has already experienced the pain of absence from people and places. But it is a "love of absence" since her heart and soul yearn to be absent here in order to be present there. Absent she will love her Domremy and her Meuse all the more, but young as she is, her heart has already learned how to love those who are absent and far away. This is the "strange love of absence" which must be a part of Joan's character if she is to fulfill her destiny. She suffers by being present because she is convinced she ought to be elsewhere, but she already knows that, being absent, she will taste the bitter nostalgia of absence. In fact, she has tasted it in advance and it is no less bitter nor less sweet than reality itself.

At the end of the third play, *Rouen,* Joan must say farewell neither to people nor places but to all people and places and life itself, another kind of absence:

Les cloches sonneront pour moi le glas des morts.

Alors la flamme embrasera ma chair vivante,
La flamme me mordra pour ma douleur humaine,
Me mangera ma chair pour ma douleur humaine:

Tel sera mon passage à la flamme infernale
Et ma douleur avant la douleur éternelle,

En la suprême, alors, des partances humaines;
Et dans mon pays on parlera longtemps de Jeanne la damneuse.

Et quand sera le jour de la colèra là,
Quand siégera le roi, le roi des épouvantes,
Quand siégera le roi pour l'effroi des vivants,

Faudra-t-il qu'à nouveau devant ce tribunal
Je sois menteuse et fausse à l'interrogatoire?
Oh je ne pourrai pas, devant ce juge-là.

Et je serai damnée à l'exil éternel,
Et je fuirai honteuse, et douloureuse, et gauche,
En l'exil infernal à jamais exilée.

Alors commencera l'étrange exil sans plage,
L'étrange exil d'absence où vous n'êtes pas là,
La savoureuse absence, et dévorante et lente
Et folle à savourer, effolante et vivante . . .

Je me sentirai folle à savourer l'absence
Et vivante en folie et folle à tout jamais . . .   (pp. 311–2)

The bells will toll the knell of death for me.

Then the flame will engulf my living flesh,
The flame will burn me in my human sorrow,
Will eat my flesh in my human sorrow:

Such will be my passage into the eternal flame
And my sorrow in the face of eternal sorrow,

In the supreme of human departures, then;
And in my country one will long speak of Joan the damner.

And when the day of wrath has arrived,
When the king holds court, the king of terror,
When the king holds court to the horror of the living,

Will it be necessary that again before this tribunal
I be a liar and false in the questioning?
Oh I cannot, before that judge.

And I shall be damned to eternal exile,
And I shall flee ashamed, and sorrowful, and awkward,
Exiled forever in the infernal exile.

Then will begin this strange exile without shores,
The strange exile of absence in which you are not there,
The savory absence, and devouring and slow
And maddening to taste, bewildering and living . . .

I shall feel myself crazy to savor the absence
And living in madness and mad forever . . .

Death will thus be this "strange exile of absence in which [one is] not there." The world and all the people in it will still be there but one will be absent, suffering the flames of eternal damnation while savoring this infernal exile in madness. It is no longer the world which is absent to one but one who is absent to the world in an exile without shores, a place to which no one returns because he can never leave it, a place to savor for eternity. Joan has not yet found the resolution of her dilemma. Although resigned to the necessity of dying, she is not yet ready to die without a reason.

Such was the attitude of the non-believing half-believer Péguy in 1897. By 1910 he had found his faith again and reworked his drama of Joan, blowing fifteen pages up into one hundred fifty in the form of *Le Mystère de la charité de Jeanne d'Arc.* Here Joan finds her reason for dying. Because of her difference Joan feels herself estranged and isolated from others. We no longer want to believe in Péguy's maxim according to which "In order to kill war, one must make war" (pp. 33, 393), an idea that marked the period before World War I and which that war did not succeed in validating. But Joan realizes that in order to eliminate the present suffering, it would be necessary to add to that suffering. In the face of this necessity she feels herself very much present in the world, but because of her destiny, the world is absent to her. It is no longer she who is absent but others. As she states in a dialogue with Madame Gervaise:

> —Tous ceux-là que j'aimais sont absents de moi-même.
> —Même Dieu. C'est cela, tous.
> —*Tous* ceux que j'aimais sont absents de moi.   (p. 424)

> —All those I loved are absent from me.
> —Even God. That's it, all.
> —*All* those I loved are absent from me.

Even God has abandoned her in her necessity to cause suffering. She finally resolves her dilemma: her reason for being and for dying will be charity, the sacrifice of herself to the evil she must do for the good of others. She will be able to save others from eternal absence through her own absence. The sacrifice of self will give reason to the unreasonable and put an end to the absence of others.

The pages on night and sleep in *Le Porche du mystère de la deuxième vertu* (The Portico of the Mystery of the Second

Virtue) of 1911 are among the most beautiful on the subject in French literature. Sleep becomes another kind of absence, the temporary absence which repairs and restores, this absence that is a gift of God, His "most beautiful creation" (p. 663). But the poet also thinks of his children and of the time when he will be absent from them:

> Il pense avec tendresse à ce temps où il ne sera plus,
> Parce que n'est-ce pas on ne peut pas être toujours
> On ne peut pas être et avoir été.   (p. 546)

> He thinks with tenderness of that time when he will no
>   longer be.
> Because is it not so that one cannot be forever
> One cannot be and have been.

This last line would seem more original if one had not already encountered it in Balzac's *Eugénie Grandet* of 1833. In any event, the children will be alone in the world and he will be the great absent one. The tone of these allusions has become more personal, less historical, more intimate, less theatrical, and at the same time more general. According to the natural destiny of man, children take the place of the father and one can say that they are present by means of his absence.

If Péguy thought of his own absence in relation to his children in *Le Porche*, he thought of the absence of his friends in relation to himself in the "Présentation de la Beauce à Notre Dame de Chartres" of 1913. Was he thinking of the quantity of companions he had alienated over the years when he wrote about "our absent friends and our depopulated hearts" (*nos amis absents et nos coeurs dépeuplés*, p. 896)? He had sacrificed many friendships to his principles. Was he beginning to miss those friends? "Absent friends" can be simply dead friends, those who disappear inevitably in life. As I said earlier, one can attempt to depopulate his heart in order to make room for divine grace, but in the fifth prayer, "Prière de déférence," Pèguy writes: "So many friends turned away from this solitary heart" (*Tant d'amis détournés de ce coeur solitaire*, p. 922). Friends turned away by whom and by what? The depopulated heart has become the "solitary heart" and the reader must ask himself the question, through the will or the fault of whom? The ambiguity renders all the more agonizing this solitude in which love and fidelity are not yet dead but have become completely useless without friends.

In Péguy's final work *Eve* of 1913, he speaks of the absence suffered by those who are killed in war, calling them, as noted previously: "Happy are those who have died for the carnal earth, / But provided it was in a just war" (*Heureux ceux qui sont morts pour la terre charnelle, / Mais pourvu que ce fût dans une juste guerre*, p. 1028). We no longer believe so strongly in the possibility of "just wars" while super-patriotism is no longer quite so fashionable. The world has become too small for countries to be able to afford this sentiment which separates more than it unites. Péguy himself suffered from "an obsessive fear: that of dying too late,"[3] which perhaps explains how his feeling for absence was both nostalgia for the past and an anticipation of the future. The forty year old did not want to become a fifty year old. One understands why Péguy prayed God to place "a few grams of earth" (*quelques grammes de terre*, p. 1030) with the dead in their grave so that they might feel a little less their "eternal absence."

As for Péguy himself, he is never more present to us than through his absence, through his heroic death. In this sense, Péguy's death, one month and five days after the beginning of World War I, brought traditional French poetry to its end. In the same way, Apollinaire's death, two days before the end of World War I, announced the beginning of modern French poetry. To measure the distance that separates these two poets, one has only to compare "Adieu, Meuse" with "Le Pont Mirabeau." If Apollinaire remains present to us through his demanding presence, Péguy remains present to us through his absence, by "this strange reinforcement of presence by absence."

CHAPTER 9

The Literary Critic

PÉGUY'S literary criticism is so dispersed among his numerous
essays that it is difficult to locate and isolate. The reader frequently has trouble establishing the connection between such
criticism and the apparent subject of the essay. Nevertheless, to
isolate the criticism from its context does violence to Péguy's
thought and runs the risk of falsifying his "message." The risk
must be taken, however, if we are going to get a clearer view of
his evaluations of his predecessors and contemporaries that include Sophocles, Pascal, Corneille, Racine, Hugo, Taine, Renan,
and Zola, to name a few.

I The Ancients: A Greek Dramatist

Among the ancient Greeks Péguy quotes the dramatist
Sophocles at greatest length. Taking his *Antigone* as an example
in 1900 (*O* I, pp. 195–7), he finds the heroine's lamentations
pagan but related to Christian lamentations, the condemnation
by Creon indicative of future Christian damnations, and the
description of hell by the chorus similar to the Christian concept of hell. Nevertheless, no matter how formidable Péguy
found such lamentations and consolations, he could not compare
them to the Christian imagination for "The pagans, who loved
life and beauty, were never able nor did they want to succeed in
creating such horrors. There must be at the bottom of Christian
sentiment a frightening complicity, a hideous complacency in
sickness and death" (p. 198). Péguy had to admit, however,
that these lamentations and consolations were probably as
frightening for the Athenians who witnessed the play as
Christian concepts are for the modern believer, for "There is a
great distance between tragic sorrow and the ugliness of reality."

As mentioned in Chapter Three, Péguy's essay "The Parallel

126

Supplicants" of 1905 (pp. 869–935) is based on an extended comparison between the supplications in Sophocles' *OEdipus the King* and those of the Russian workers to their tsar. In addition to these ideas, Péguy insists on the impossibility of translation (p. 890), for like all human labor, "when one has the freshness, one does not have the competence. And when one develops a little competence, one perceives that one no longer has the freshness, which will never return, which nothing replaces, which is the foremost of qualities." Since "the supporters of the would-be scientific, modern historical methods" never pose the problem in these human terms, they are doomed to failure and their disciples are doomed never to know the real Sophocles.

According to Péguy, all great modern theories are generally only transpositions of ancient theories into a modern and sometimes Christian language. If one had the time, this point could be proved but we would also learn that such theories were "generally a great deal more intelligent, . . . more subtle and more discerning" (p. 1087) as expressed by the ancients than they are by the moderns. Péguy's resigned conclusion is that we are, alas, "only poor moderns."

While Péguy maintains in an unpublished essay of 1909 that almost anyone can find in a chorus of Sophocles "a sudden illumination" (*O* II, p. 246) if he proceeds by the methods of art, the moderns, who neither respect nor listen to a text, can find in the lines of almost any poet including Sophocles only a subject for accusation. Péguy did make, however, in the same essay an interesting observation about the belief of the ancients in their gods, a point that could reorient one's thinking about Greek tragedy: "For the Greeks it does indeed seem, since Homer, and all the more reason since the tragic writers, (and when I speak of tragic writers I speak only of Aeschylus and Sophocles, I naturally do not speak of that contemptible Euripides), it does indeed seem that Olympus, that the gods are already beings of mythology. Not that they do not believe in them. But they believe in them with a faith that is so to speak only mythological itself" (p. 257). Already in Homer Péguy discerned a certain disdain and unconscious envy of the gods since the latter, being immortal, risked nothing (p. 261). Thus Olympus was not intimately linked to the world of the Greeks, but superimposed on it. Still, Sophocles demonstrated that a sort of extreme unction was the most import sacrament for the pagan, just as it is for the Christian, since it comes last (p. 439).

Péguy made one of his last and most interesting observation about Sophocles in 1914. Commenting on Julien Benda's criticism of Bergsonism as "a pathetic [*pathétique*] philosophy," Péguy rushes to the defense of the pathetic, asserting that "there is an intellectualism of the pathetic as there is an intellectualism of logic, or of mathematics. . . ." (p. 1317). Just as comedy is not inferior to tragedy, so passion is not necessarily inferior to reason. The proof is to be found in Sophocles: "As for the tragic I confess that I see nothing human that is superior to the *pathetic* of Sophocles . . . there is in this *pathetic* . . . a *knowledge*, a thorough analysis of nature, of the reality of man and of fatality." The reader would be more impressed by Péguy's acute insight if he could forget that Péguy had maintained in 1910 that he had found "all of Sophocles" (p. 837) in two lines from Barrès' eulogy of the poet Jean Moréas. This rapid contraction and expansion of Péguy's vision is one of his most exasperating and frequently most illuminating characteristics.

II *The "Ancients": A French Thinker*

From his essay in the first issue of the *Cahiers* of January 1900 to the issue of April 1914, Péguy never ceases to praise Pascal. Some of his most significant remarks about the seventeenth-century thinker are also contained in his posthumous essays. The title of the first essay, "Letter from a Provincial," was borrowed from Pascal's famous *Letters to a Provincial.* In the following issue Péguy mentions Pascal's "Prayer Asking God for the Good Use of Illnesses" and expresses his admiration for Pascal's "religious passion and, to speak plainly, this passionately geometric faith, geometrically passionate, so absolutely exact, so absolutely proper, so absolutely punctual, so perfect, so infinitely finite, so well made, so well closed and uniformly painful and consoled, in the end so ultimately faithful and so practically confident, so foreign to us" (*O* I, p. 126). As so frequently happens, Péguy would seem to have said too much, thus vitiating the impact of his rhetoric. He saves himself by adding that last expression "so foreign to us" which reveals the time and distance, physical and spiritual, that separate a man like Pascal from us, the victims, as Péguy would have it, of the modern world. Péguy did not reveal his return to his faith until eight years later but from the beginning he "maintained for this Christian a strange uneasy admiration" (p. 126) that he never lost. In his essay of March 1900, "Still Concerning the Grippe," he quotes long selections from the story of Pascal's life and death as recounted by Pascal's sister (pp. 162–71), finding consolation in Pascal's stoic faith in the face of sickness and death. The essay constitutes one of Péguy's earliest lessons on the uses of good reading.

In 1900 he drew the comparison between religious faith and Socialism, mentioned earlier in Chapter Two. If a man of the intellectual stature of Pascal and a humble woman could both die united in their firm faith, why could not the Socialist ideas of the intellectuals become a firm part of the political faith of simple citizens (p. 174)? Such was Péguy's hope. His feeling was that Pascal's doctors were not ignorant like those in a Molière play; they simply did not know what we know today because of Pascal's *Thoughts*. Furthermore, Pascal suffered from the equally fatal twin diseases of believing and thinking (p. 179). After an extended quotation from the *Thoughts* (pp. 183–8) and a brief one from Racine, Péguy concludes his essay with a rapier thrust at the anticlericals who were closing schools and outlawing religious orders—that is, limiting the freedom of others.

Péguy refers again to Pascal in 1900 on the subject of the mortality and immortality of the soul (p. 222), maintaining that more frequent and longer quotations from Pascal would have helped clarify the dilemma. Finally, he quotes Pascal's wonderful observation about natural style that reveals not an author but a man while those of good taste expect to find a man but are surprised to find an author. Péguy, being less demanding than Pascal, hoped that his readers would find his style natural and would regard him as a simple author who practiced his trade honestly and conscientiously.

Péguy did not hesitate to compare himself to "this inglorious Pascal" (p. 263) who would, like him, have asked for the

definitions of words before any discussion. This remark was made
in 1900. Complaining again about the mechanical teaching and
learning methods of the obligatory lay schools in 1902, Péguy
insisted that it was by reading Pascal, among many others, that
a man is formed and not by reciting manuals by rote (p. 536).
Nor did he hesitate to quote Pascal while writing about the fear-
less Zola, also in 1902. One had only to look more closely to
discern "the good things" Zola had done and which he had done
simply and naturally in the spirit of Pascal.

Péguy claimed perhaps too much in 1904 by stating that "a
single word of Pascal" would have annihilated the enormous
Dialogues of Renan (p. 720). The French as heirs of Pascal
should learn that "eternal salvation is of an infinitely infinite
price" (p. 939) as demonstrated by Louis de Gonzague in the
essay of that name of 1905. They should know, as Péguy noted
the following year, that "an essential thinker like Pascal" (p.
1007) is one of those great men who are geniuses and thus
reveal again that genius is of a different order from talent.

In a posthomous essay Péguy underlines the necessity of
analyzing word by word a remark like that of Pascal's according to which "man is neither angel nor beast" (*O* II, p. 394),
if one really wants to understand the human condition. Later
in the essay he repeats this idea (p. 443). So convinced was he
of the importance of Pascal's *Thoughts* that he was sure his
friend Halévy would include it among the few books he could
take with him on a military campaign.

While taking to task "A new Theologian, Mr. Fernand Laudet"
in 1911, Péguy refers him to Pascal's "Prayer for the Good Use
of Illnesses," reminding him "that saintliness, that grace operates
with a minimum of temporal matter" and that Pascal "is a
Christian author at least the equal of Mr. Anatole France" (p.
915). He also remarks that we are all as stupid (*bête*) as Pascal
(p. 972), that everyone receives the same body of Christ in
communion as Pascal (p. 973), and that when the twentieth
century wants to be fervent it does all the most ordinary things
indicated by Pascal (p. 979). He blames Rudler for having
praised Gustave Lanson in terms that we should hesitate to use
for Pascal (p. 994). Furthermore, he castigates a certain Mathieu
or Matthieu for claiming that Pascal was a forger who left no

trace (p. 996). In 1914, he asserts that "nothing is more profound than an anlysis and a criticism by Pascal" (p. 1319).

In another posthumous essay Péguy demonstrates how "the royal wisdom and the royal sorrow of King Solomon became the tragic and more than royal distress of Pascal" (p. 1370) and that religion, Jewish or Christian, is not reserved for extraordinary beings but is for the most common of us all, as Pascal would say (p. 1371). According to Péguy, "Jesus was unable (or did not wish) to graft Jewish patience on the Christian body. That was also necessary, doubly necessary in order to produce a Pascal, in order to realize this well of distress, this desert of sand, this abyss of melancholy" (p. 1373). Corneille's play *Polyeucte* differs greatly "from a certain tendency of Pascal. It renders to the temporal its due" (p. 1445). Nevertheless, it is Pascal who defines "stoicism and a certain epicurean scepticism as the two poles of thought and system of the ancient world . . . from the Christian point of view" (p. 1450). Pascal also went "to the very heart of the debate," having seen that "stoicism gave, was charged with giving the maximum of ancient grandeur *sub specie,* from the point of view of Christian grandeur, the maximum of nature from the point of view of receiving grace, the maximum of the hero (and of the martyr), from the point of view of the saint and the martyr, the maximum of man in God from the point of view of God, the maximum of the world in God from the point of view of God" (p. 1451).

Thus ends Péguy's eulogy of Pascal. If, in this last quotation as in the first, Péguy verges on claiming too much for Pascal, his many references to the seventeenth-century thinker do reveal that Pascal's thought was for him a living, integral, and necessary part of his own thought. He had learned from Pascal and was eager to teach his readers the many possible good uses of good reading of a great author who was tortured and tormented by his own inadequacies but who never abandoned his faith.

III   *The "Ancients": Two French Dramatists*

Péguy makes trenchant observations about the plays of all three of France's greatest seventeenth-century playwrights, Corneille, Molière, and Racine. As early as 1902 he classed both Corneille and Racine among those authors who are essential to the formation of a man (*O* I, p. 536); but by 1905 Corneille had become "the greatest of all" (p. 822). Corneille retained this position in Péguy's eyes, for he alone among the three was worthy to be placed in the ranks of Rembrandt, Beethoven, Pascal, and Michelet (p. 1007).

If Péguy wrote less about Molière, he nevertheless identified sufficiently with Alceste in *Le Misanthrope* to find the dramatist to be a true Dreyfusite, as a recent critic points out.[1] But the character he identified with most intimately was Corneille's heroic Polyeucte. His identification was so strong that he rendered this character from a play the symbol, the image, and the "mythic figure" of his own destiny.[2] In a posthumous essay of 1909 Péguy states that "to speak of Corneille and *Polyeucte . . .* I need rolls of paper, to the extent of exhausting all the forests of the world. And I shall depopulate the forests of the earth. And there will be no more cellulose" (*O* II, p. 240). From Péguy's lengthy digressions on the subject, the reader is sometimes convinced that he was well on his way to succeeding.

By 1910 Péguy began to focus more closely on Corneille. If he made general statements like "*honor* in Corneille is a sort of *proper* name. It is a name of a person, a name of some one. Whom one knows very well" (p. 718), he also subjected Corneilles' rhymes in -*ort,* including *mort* (death), *sort* (destiny), *effort,* and *port,* to close scrutiny, revealing the several nuances and the unexpected effects Corneille could achieve by such simple means (pp. 720-4). In the same essay Péguy draws up his long parallel between Corneille and Racine (pp. 772-807). He had already made the revealing observation: "The wounds we receive we find in Racine. The beings we are we find in Corneille" (p. 770). He goes on to say that Corneille's plays are full of grace while Racine's are full of disgrace, Corneille's filled with salvation and Racine's with perdition, Corneille's with order, Racine's with disorder. According to him "Racine was never able to create a gracious being, not even Bérénice" (p. 773) and "The victims in Racine are themselves more cruel than the executioners in Corneille" (p. 775). He insists that Racine's "men are women, they all suffer from feminine contamination, from some feminine contamination. They are all emasculated, and it is this very feminine cruelty one finds in them" (p. 777). I suppose Péguy would have classified Hamlet as a Racinian man. If he called Racine "this great psychologist" (p. 781), he also described Racine's plays as a "numerical series" in which one play is simply added to another without building to a climax, as do the late plays of Corneille. For Péguy Racine's plays are only variations on a theme. Evidently Péguy could not distinguish between the psychology of an Andromaque, a Bérénice, an Iphigénie, or a Phèdre, leading him to maintain somewhat ambiguously that "On the whole he [Racine] always wrote the same tragedy, which was always a pure masterpiece" (pp. 782-3).

Péguy was, however, also able to say good things about Racine: "Hundreds, thousands of lines assail me on all sides, so pure, so beautiful, so harmonious; more than Virgilian; even so melodious; of such a line, of such fullness, of such beauty; of such a sweep; so perfect; of such accomplishment; so perfectly pure so perfectly beautiful" (p. 785). Unfortunately such hyperbole and wholesale approval hardly constitute literary criticism since Péguy would go to even greater lengths where Corneille was concerned. He was certain that "a first career, the great, the greatest of all tragic careers, the greatest of all dramatic careers, certainly the greatest even of all poetic careers came to an end, crowned itself in *Polyeucte*" (p. 802). And Shakespeare? As early as 1907 Péguy spoke of "this *Polyeucte* (and this Pauline) to whom, to which nothing is comparable in the history of the world" (*O* I, p. 1203). In the posthumous essay Péguy left unfinished at his death, he continues in the same vein, insisting that "the profane tragedy in *Polyeucte* is the fullest and the purest and the most ancient and the profoundest and, if I may say so, at the same time the most gracious and gravest and most sacred profane tragedy of love and honor that we have" (*O* II, p. 1449). It was obviously such extravagant observations that led one critic to remark on "the delirious praise Péguy lavished on *Polyeucte*."[3] No one would deny that *Polyeucte* is a masterpiece but when the critic identifies too closely with his subject, be it a character or a whole play, his vision becomes blurred and his judgment dulled. A recent critic has done an excellent job of separating the grain from the chaff in Péguy's criticism of Corneille.[4] Yet one fears that the general reader be-

comes impatient with such extravagance and thus discounts the
many penetrating and revealing remarks Péguy does make about
Corneille and his play, particularly since these statements are
dispersed through literally hundreds of pages of prose. A close
study can help us, however, to get to know better "this country
they call Corneille" (p. 1177).

IV An "Ancient" "Modern": A French Poet

Péguys favorite poet is without doubt Victor Hugo. He gives
more attention in greater depth to this nineteenth-century giant
than to any other French author, Corneille included. His judgments are in general more tempered than those he lavishes on
the seventeenth-century dramatist. This result is perhaps due to
Péguy's early rejection of Hugo as an enormously successful poet.
For several reasons, Péguy later found Hugo to be a true, that
is, "ancient" voice of France. Yet, in the end, Péguy condemned
Hugo for his overweening ambition.

As early as 1900 Péguy inveighed against Hugo stating "We
know how much demagogic lying and baseness there was be-
neath the exaggerated glory" that was Hugo's (*O* I, p. 262).
Péguy even protested against the use of *gloire* (honor and reputation) to refer to both Hugo and Tolstoy (p. 263). As a con-
firmed Socialist, Péguy in 1902 found Hugo's reputation to be
entirely false: "One wants to make us believe that Hugo was
the poet of the humble. And truly, he was the most shameless
exploiter of them. Never before Hugo had a bourgeois so shame-
lessly exploited the revolting description of misery in order to
secure luxury, power, and money" (p. 469). Hugo could hardly
have been called a Socialist but then was Shakespeare exploiting
the insane in his *King Lear?* In 1904 Péguy found Hugo "so
eternal every time he didn't attempt to have an idea of his
own" (p. 737).

But in 1905 Péguy's attitude towards Hugo began to change.
While strolling among the Parisian crowds who were anticipating
the parade to celebrate the visit by the king of Spain, Péguy
thought to himself how "curiously" one's mind inevitably turned to
Hugo during such great state ceremonial events. Péguy took the
occasion to expatiate at length on Hugo (pp. 818–48), noting that

the poet brought together Notre-Dame, the Pantheon, and the Invalides, and the religious, intellectual, creative, and military genius of France. Already he found *Les Châtiments* (*Chastisements*) "the most ardent of his works, the greatest perhaps and the strongest, perhaps the only sincere, absolutely" (p. 823), another idea to which he would adhere faithfully for the rest of his life. But he also wrote at length of the rhythm of Hugo's poetry, the rhymes, the assonances and consonances, the movement, the architecture, the design, the visual and auditory images, in a passage which is one of the more acute criticisms of Hugo's poetry, including the bad poetry. Still, he could not forgive Hugo for being a pacifist only when pacificism was popular (p. 828) nor for not having written a single successful poem on peace except for "Booz endormi" (p. 832).

By 1906 it dawned on Péguy that Hugo was indeed a Romantic (p. 1067) much as Péguy himself was, although he would have been the last to admit it. By the following year he was even content to place Hugo on a level with Michelet, calling them both "great fellows [*bougres*]" who were happy "because they were doing something" (p. 1191). Then in 1909 he found the formula of the Beatitudes in Hugo's poetry (*O* II, p. 30) that he was to use so successfully in *Eve*. He also realized that while Leconte de Lisle had grown old as an old man (*vieillard*) with a monocle and an Olympian demeanor, Hugo had grown old as an old man (*vieux*) in the peasant sense of the word (p. 134) with "eyes the most profoundly seeing that ever opened on the carnal world" (p. 135). But then Péguy slipped into the hyperbole that became, unfortunately, the hallmark of his literary criticism: "In all the books of the world, you know, there is not in the books of humanity, a single book which is certainly as pamphleteering, as polemical, and certainly as lyric, if not tragic, but perhaps as epic as *Les Châtiments* of Hugo" (p. 136).

With that Péguy was off on his long (pp. 133–215) comparison of the two versions of "Malbroug s'en va-t-en guerre" by Hugo and Beaumarchais, noting that Hugo's thirteen rhymes in *-ère* were much more faithful and telling than the rhymes in *-aine* of Beaumarchais. In the midst of this discussion Péguy turned his attention to Hugo's poem "Booz endormi," another of his favorites, commenting on its rhymes, rhythm, and most of all, its sonority, "one of the greatest sonorities the most profoundly and most totally successful in itself and in its genre and speaking absolutely" (p. 145). The repeated use of the word "absolutely" is revealing. Péguy was absolute in his religious faith and in his political faith, and yet the reader gets the impression from Péguys excessive verbiage that he was not really that absolutely sure about anything except his own convictions which were hardly endorsed by the church or the party.

Péguy found that a whole thesis could be written on the role of the assassin in Hugo's works while the guillotine assumed "a romantic grandeur" (p. 147) that was difficult to explain. In fact, Hugo's short novel "The Last Day of a Condemned Man" exerted a capital influence "on the literary, political, romantic, humanitarian career of Victor Hugo, and not only on his career but on his work itself" (pp. 147–8). After these macabre observations Péguy made an analysis of Hugo's version of "Malbroug s'en va-t-en guerre' with enough formulae to make one think of contemporary Structuralist criticism with its many would-be mathematical diagrams. But the Structuralists might well heed Péguy's warning that "one creates symbols with great difficulty. Then, provided one does not use symbols, one understands immediately" (p. 151). To understand Hugo today one would need, as Péguy points out, "a dictionary of proper names" (p. 207), so vast was Hugo's knowledge. And if his play *Les Burgraves* was only "a book of history" (p. 269), Péguy came to realize that Hugo was an "ancient" rather than a "modern" because he "saw the world as if it had just been created" (p. 313).

By 1910 Péguy had decided that Hugo "was perhaps on the whole a badly ambitious Classical writer who in order to succeed, clothed himself, made himself up like a Romantic" (p. 719), a point he made at least three times (pp. 713, 1351). Because there was not a single Racinian line to be found in Hugo but much that was Corneillian, he analyzed at great length (pp. 728–63) Hugo's poem "Booz endormi" finding Hugo not a Christian but a pagan (p. 743) who "had received the gift of seeing creation as if it had left this morning the hands of the Creator" (p. 747). But in the end Péguy could not forgive Hugo along with Napoleon as the two representatives of the "hypocrisy of pacifism" (p. 864) and by 1914 Péguy was again excoriating

Hugo for his ambition, for his fear of "failing in his temporal career" (p. 1353).

Thus Péguy's criticism of Hugo was in many respects the most profound of his career, revealing a true comprehension of the enormity of Hugo's creation while regretting that the man passed through so many metamorphoses. One critic gives us a brief but clear view of this evolution of Péguy's attitude towards Hugo[5] while a second gives us a fuller view of the same subject.[6] Péguy perhaps never again reaches the heights of true literary criticism as he does in his several lengthy analyses of only a few of Hugo's seemingly endless works.

V *The "Moderns": Two French Historians*

One of the authors Péguy quotes at greatest length is the philosopher-historian Ernest Renan. While writing about him Péguy mentions, as almost every critic does, the historian and literary historian Hippolyte Taine. Taine was almost an exact contemporary of Renan and, according to Péguy, was an exponent of the same kind of "modern" ideas. Péguy held these two men jointly responsible in great part for the degeneration of the "modern" world.

Yet Péguy's attitude towards Renan, at least, was not always entirely negative. As early as 1900 he admired but distrusted Renan, noting that his *Dialogues* "have a strange charm and a marvelous inconsistency, an admirable continuation from the accepted idea to the unacceptable idea" (*O* I, p. 144), that they are an unusual amalgam of "the entirely false formula" and "the entirely true certitude" (p. 145). Under Renan's "apparent humility" lurked a "presumptuous authority" that could only lead to all kinds of tyranny since he maintained that education must be reserved for the elite in order to produce great men who alone produce great works and thus further progress. In addition, Renan failed to define his terms, thus leading Péguy to admit that "this Renan would make me love pedantry" (p. 156). In 1900 Péguy was almost equidistant in time from his loss of faith around 1891 and the recovery of his faith in 1908 so that he could write, "Let us believe that a true suffering is not comparable to the best of false enchantments. Let's not be religious, even with Renan" (p. 1557).

A few months later Péguy pondered Renan's politics or perhaps better, his political philosophy. He wondered why Renan had not become or remained a Socialist, a fact which could naturally be attributed to his character and background, but which Péguy also attributed to his having "understood badly what he himself had said." The idea is a dangerous one for the critic to push too far but Péguy, in an unusual turn of thought, notes that Renan had not "really understood personally as a spectator the character that he had dramatically put forward for us" (p. 256). The answer is, of course, that one does not usually fully understand the character one projects and frequently it is only after one has left a scene that others can give a true shape to one's character. Nevertheless, Corneille, Racine, and Renan, whom Péguy would also list among the "great dramatic poets," have all disappeared in history. "However, the characters they bequeathed us are still living among us, active among us" (p. 257). Just as Corneille forgot his Polyeucte, and Racine his Phèdre, so Renan forgot his Socialist character. He may not have been an active Socialist but his example led a great many others to the idea of Socialism. In this sense Péguy could say that "The republic thus represented by Mr. Renan is also my republic."

But Renan's "elitism" rankled Péguy. As early as 1901 he was convinced that "an omnipotent government of intellectuals" as foreseen by Renan was unreasonable and illogical (p. 410). He criticized Renan for insisting that humanity would become God (p. 700), and that it would know all there is to know about its past in a century. Péguy quite rightly maintains that humanity can never know its past completely since humanity, in order to do so, would have to be the last humanity. Of course, once last, there would be no more humanity to know its past. Péguy also found Renan's ideas of natural science "monstrous" (p. 707). Renan asserted that the superior beings to come would use man as man has used animals. This act would provoke man to realize "that man uses animals badly" (p. 708). Péguy rejected this concept—he had already assigned a specific place to animals as adolescents in "The Harmonious City." Péguy could not accept Renan's grisly ideas on human vivisection either, the sacrifice of a living being to some end legitimized by what Renan called "nature" (p. 710). Most of Renan's ideas have been disproved precisely "by the sciences in which Renan thought to find his most solid support, by the physical, chemical sciences, particularly by the natural sciences" (p. 720).

Péguy then made a distinction that later allowed him to absolve and thus save at least part of Renan's thought. The *Dialogues* are, according to him "a metaphysical text," "a theological text" (p. 722). Taine's work, *La Fontaine and His Fables,* is a product of the same "modern" spirit as that of Renan but is characterized by an "inflexible and crude assurance." Péguy could not forgive Taine for his pretentions of having penetrated "all the operations of genius itself" as well as "the secret of nature and man" (p. 724). Péguy insisted on "his unintelligence and his heresy, his crudeness, his ignorance" and most of all, "his presumption" (p. 728). Compared to Taine, Renan was "more informed, more philosopher, more artist, more man of the world" (p. 729). Renan was thus able "to form a distant superhumanity into an all knowing God through a totalization of historical memory" (p. 730). Although Renan's system was similar to Taine's and to that of the "modern" world, there was a subtle but important difference between them. Renan's superhumanity would usurp "the functions of divine knowledge" while Taine's schemes would usurp "the functions of divine production." Renan's scientism would only attempt to arrive at the omniscience of God while Taine's intention was to appropriate the whole idea of divine creation. Another distinction is that Taine is operating in the present while Renan's usurpation is placed safely in a distant future (p. 734). Renan's works thus rise to the level of metaphysical meditation while Taine's operate on the level of would-be demonstrated or demonstrable scientific certainty.

By 1906 Péguy decided that Taine and Renan were "not as qualified and professional historians as they thought" (p. 995); but again Péguy drew a distinction. The reader finds in Renan's works great metaphysical meditation tinged with a certain sadness. As Péguy remarks, Renan's "occupations as historian and his preoccupations as philosopher did not communicate at all between themselves" (p. 1009). Thus while his history may have become outmoded, his metaphysical preoccupations never will (p. 1013). Frankly, Renan disdained the "moderns" (p. 1041) and while the inauguration of Renan's statue in his home town of Tréguier was a vulgar display completely foreign to Renan's character, he must be held responsible, nevertheless, for his part in creating this "modern" world which could dream up such a ceremony. Also, one must not forget that *The Future of Science* is "the foundation book of the superstition of modern science" (p. 1054). Péguy was probably again claiming and blaming Renan for too much, but he may have been at least partially right where French thought is concerned.

Although Péguy claimed in 1907 that Taine and Renan "will never cease to accompany us" (p. 1146), as assuredly the influence, at least of Renan, certainly did, the two historians practically disappeared from the pages of the *Cahiers* if not from Péguy's mind during the last seven years of his life. The configuration of Péguy's relations with Renan has been clearly set forth in a recent article,[7] but more undoubtedly remains to be said on the subject. Some critics still maintain with some justice that Taine "is truly a great historian of art and literature"[8] while others claim at least as much for Renan. In a sense, both Taine and Renan have been consumed by their own subject, history, whose evolution has left them somewhat behind. They both had great minds and produced great works that must be taken into consideration in almost any evaluation of nineteenth-century France; but neither one is, in all of his ramifications, an example to be followed. Péguys contention that Renan will endure because of his metaphysical meditations must still stand the test of time.

VI The "Moderns": A French Novelist

In January 1898 the novelist Emile Zola took his courageous stand in the Dreyfus Affair by publishing his "Letter to the President of the Republic," better known under the title "J'accuse!" The following month Péguy published an article in a Socialist journal titled "Homage to Zola by Young Writers." Late in 1899 his only other essay devoted entirely to the novelist appeared in *Le Mouvement socialiste* (The Socialist Movement). Péguy felt strongly enough about this second article to republish it in its original form in the *Cahiers* in December 1902. Péguy was thus attracted to Zola primarily because of his role in the Affair, but he also had some pertinent things to say about the man and one of his novels.

Between January 1898 and September 1899 Zola published at least six articles relating to the Dreyfus Affair as well as his novel *Fecundity,* the first of his projected *Four Gospels.* Moved by Zola's forceful declarations and creative powers, Péguy had to see for himself just what kind of man Zola really was. By that time the novelist was rich and famous, thus Péguy found him comfortably ensconced "in his wealthy bourgeois house" (*O* I, p. 538). But the man himself turned out to be quite different from Péguy's expectations. Péguy's portrait is well worth quoting:

The man I found was not a bourgeois, but a dark peasant, grown old, grey, his features drawn, withdrawn within him, a plowman of books, an aligner of furrows, a solid, robust, stubborn man with shoulders as round and strong as a Roman arch, rather small and not very voluminous, like the peasants of Central France . . . He had what peasants have that is without doubt most beautiful, that equable air, that equanimity more invincible than the perpetuity of the earth. He was stocky. He was tired. He had an ordinary, easygoing assurance. He had an admirable powerlessness to be astonished by what he did, an extraordinary freshness to be astonished at what others did that was ugly, evil, and nasty. (pp. 538–9)

Péguy was obviously impressed by this great man who was to die tragically three years later at the age of sixty-two.

In their conversation Zola expressed his sadness over the Socialists' abandonment of "the rare defenders of justice." Zola's observation may have rightly applied to government representatives, journalists, and even Socialist leaders, but Péguy was convinced that it did not apply to the workers. Péguy never saw Zola again, but he praised "the beautiful classical order" and the "beautiful writing" of the conclusion of Zola's "Letter to the President." He was certain that it was "one of the most beautiful literary monuments we have" (p. 540) and as far as journalistic rhetoric is concerned, he may well be right. He found the letter a "beautiful prophecy, since human prophecy does not consist of imagining a future, but of depicting to one-

self the future as if it were already the present." He did not find
Zola's repetitions or variations "artificial" but a good example of
what must be said and said again. Sincerity was Zola's profoundest characteristic, "the very foundation of his always
young naiveté." Péguy would try to use repetitions and variations
in the future which were not always, perhaps, as successful as
those of Zola. The idea of this youthful outlook Péguy developed
in somewhat different way when speaking of Hugo, as we have
seen.

But for the moment in his comparisons between Zola and Hugo
the latter came out the loser. The critic Gustave Kahn had
already noticed the difference between "the leadership of a moral
order, rather than literary" that Zola exercized and that exerted
by Hugo near the end of his life. Péguy found that while the
effect was the same, the spirit was totally different. Hugo left
Péguy with an impression of insincerity, of an authoritarian leadership, which meant that Zola "was what Hugo never was, a
protagonist" (p. 541). In his enthusiasm Péguy may have sold
Hugo a bit short, but it gave him an excellent opening for his
criticism of Zola's novel, *Fecundity*.

As one might expect, at this stage in Péguy's life his interpretation was initially political and sociological. Reading the novel
in serial form in the newspaper, he had hoped that its hero would
prove to be a Socialist, and the book "the gospel of Socialism."
Instead, after a modest beginning, the hero becomes the worst of
capitalists "exercizing the right of use and abuse on an in-
calculable number of the means of production" (p. 542). He had
reared "a bourgeois race" since children must produce more than
they consume if they are not to become parasites on society.
Fecundity was "a conservative book, indifferent to the wage-
earning class as the Gospel of Jesus was indifferent to slavery"
(p. 544).

The moralizer Péguy soon takes over. Although the book is "a
love story," it is not "a book of peace and goodness" (p. 546),
nor "a book of charity" (p. 547), nor "a book of goodness, of
humanity" (p. 548), nor "a book of peace" but "a book of war,"
"the book of the conquest of humanity" (p. 550) by its bourgeois
characters. How and why a revolutionary like Zola "did not
became a Socialist" (p. 551) mystifies and saddens Péguy. In

spite of this fact Péguy still finds something to admire in the book: its "classical order" (p. 552), the absence of artifice in its style, its "profound rhythm," the repetitions that are new beginnings, its "classical sincerity." He finds its author "impassive like nature, patient like her, and for those who don't know, boring like her" (pp. 552–3), an acute capsule critique of at least one aspect of Zola the man and his works. Péguy disputes several of the details of both the domestic and political economy of the novel as well as its psychology. Zola excels in describing good and evil but somehow they merely exist side by side in his novels, revealing nothing of "their strange, their mysterious kinship" that they have in life. Zola was still a captive of the old theory of the association of ideas (p. 555). He had not read Bergson and was thus unaware of the recent and more subtle theories, rendering his psychology crude and mechanical. Péguy concluded by stating that "*Fecundity* is not an absolutely successful average work, but a superior work contestable in many regards and which leaves [the reader with] a great deal of sadness" (pp. 555–6). The novel is certainly not one of the most read of Zola's works today but the judgment remains fairly accurate.

Péguy deplored the lesson of ugliness learned from Zola's works, all the more so because of the incredible number of copies in print which Péguy very carefully listed. Although Zola had acquired a literary, political, and social as well as financial fortune through his genius, he had not hesitated to publish his "Letter" which converted many readers to a desire for justice in the Dreyfus Affair. In an addendum Péguy drew up a corrected list of the number of copies of Zola's books in print and came to a total of over two million. Always suspicious of too much success, Péguy seems to be envious. Péguy intended to write articles, which never appeared, on *Work* and *Truth*, the second and third of the *Four Gospels*, while Zola himself did not live to write the fourth, *Justice*.

In 1900 Péguy was honest enough to admit that he had formerly not much liked Zola "because of the regular heaping up of his bad qualities, rather than the slow accumulation of his good qualities, [which] gave him little by little an immense popularity" (p. 263). Luckily Zola got hold of himself and made a civic gesture that brought him a "salubrious unpopularity." The following year Péguy contested Zola's concept that science is revolutionary by saying that Zola really meant that "science furnishes revolutionaries the most powerful means of revolution" and that "the application of scientific results often leads to revolutionary practices or effects. But pure science is not revolutionary" (p. 328). The idea is endlessly debatable. Péguy should, as he frequently asked others to do later, have defined his terms. Were Einstein's ideas "pure" science? Were they then not "revolutionary?" Did Péguy mean "revolutionary" uniquely in the sense of the overthrow of an existing political system? And if so, which system? Be that as it may, Péguy spoke of Zola in a meaningful way for the last time in 1904 when the death of the novelist was commemorated by, of all things, a disgusting sort of *"holy week"* which Péguy dubbed a "religious sentiment and the birth of demagogy" (p. 686). Zola had died in 1903 and the Dreyfus Affair was more or less settled in 1906, although Péguy never considered it really settled. After 1904, however, Péguy found many other subjects to discuss which is perhaps unfortunate, for Péguy might have had interesting and valid things to say about other of Zola's works.

One of Péguy's soundest and strongest statements is, thus, his literary criticism. However, this criticism, except perhaps for the better pages on Bergson, is for the most part, lost in a welter of words and has had little effect on the history of literary criticism.

CHAPTER 10

Conclusion: An Eternal Flame

THE literary criticism of Péguy's works in the sixty years since his death exhibits three main tendencies. The first, by far the most pervasive and most distressing, has been a tendency to quote from the works with no respect for chronology in order to prove a thesis, or to present Péguy as the peasant, the poet, the pamphleteer, the patriot, the prophet, and so forth. Such games are much too easy to play and neither illuminate intelligently what he says nor reveal much about the evolution of his thought or style.

A second tendency has been for those who knew him, and for some who did not, to confuse the man with his works. The reader of such criticism ends up with a glowing portrait of the author which is gainsaid on almost every other page of Péguy's essays. One of the greatest examples of this type of criticism, in a positive sense, was written by Péguy's sometime friend, collaborator, and financial mainstay of the early *Cahiers*, Romain Rolland. Rolland lists Péguy's three virtues which ensure that "he will remain, for the entire future of our people—and of all peoples—a master of life and an example."[1] The first is "the cult of honor." Yet, one wonders how significant this virtue really is. How much is Corneille read for his "cult of honor" that is mostly outmoded if not totally incomprehensible to the young people of today? Corneille is read not so much for his cult of honor as for his poetic, dynamic, and moving way of expressing the conflict between that honor and love, between "two grandeurs" as Péguy himself puts it. Unfortunately, Péguy's cult of honor now frequently seems as outmoded as that of Corneille.

Péguy's second virtue, according to Rolland, is his "fanaticism for the truth" (p. 264). Any reader of his essays is smitten by Péguy's anguish on almost every page, his frantic concern for

145

what he deems to be the truth. But his point of view was so limited, both by the circumscribed nature of his occupation as editor of the *Cahiers* and by his incessant preoccupation with his own personal concepts of what precisely constitutes the truth. Too often the truth proves to be the pet peeve of the moment and the reader is left with the uncomforable feeling that any truth, that is, any peeve which seems to become more and more monstrously petty in its development, will do and that all truths are thus disturbingly equal.

Rolland found Péguy's third virtue to be "the virtue of Hope" (p. 165). The single greatest tension created by Péguy is that between the relentless insistence on hope in his poetic works and the undeniable pessimism and inescapable death wish that begins to permeate his later essays. The reader cannot, unfortunately, always play the hope off against the pessimism. As a result he seems to find an endlessly grinding disquisition on a desperate, somewhat disconsolate, and almost despairing hope in the poetic works. This optimism contrasts with the conscious expression of an unconscious death wish that seems to proclaim Péguy's awareness of his failure as a family man, as a world-shaking or even Paris-shaking or even Left Bank-shaking editor, as a widely read and acclaimed author, as an avowed but disavowed Socialist, as a more or less self-excommunicated reconverted Catholic, as a frustrated academic, and finally as a middle-aged man with an abnormal fear of the perfectly normal fear of growing old.

Another and more recent example of this kind of criticism is one that maintains that "Péguy rediscovered in his turn the three secrets that are perhaps only one."[2] The first is "in the face of life, 'the harmonious sentiment of perfect art.'" Péguy's art, whether in his poetry or in his prose, reveals so little that is generally considered formal perfection that the reader is hard put to discover in the author any great or sustained "harmonious feeling" for perfect art. Péguy's second secret was the discovery "in himself, [of] the consciousness of the profound self" (p. 375). Péguy was so constantly torn by his own conflicting emotions, so busy venting his invective on one and all, and so intent on fulfilling his own death wish that the reader gets the impression that Péguy's "self" was very near the surface and continually on the verge of losing control of itself. The "profound self" may very well be this ceaseless war within one-self and with oneself, this war that is fought in the lucid knowledge of the inevitable end. But this concept is hardly "the harmonized self" of which Michelet speaks and which the critic finds characteristic of Péguy. The third secret was "the promise, lastly, of a City that permits everyone to contemplate this beauty and to live fraternally with the entire universe." The point of departure of Péguy's works was "The Harmonious City" and his initial vision was a fraternal one. The critic would have difficulty, however, demonstrating that this vision was sustained or developed in the subsequent works. A message of religious but hardly Socialist fraternity looms through the poetry but the author of the essays is rarely capable of harmonious and fraternal gestures except for those who were dead.

The third group of critics lays great stress on how Péguy said what he said, demonstrating how each accretion to an essay is a clever addition to and development of the basic symbolism of the text, thereby proving that Péguy had in mind a grand design that constituted the architectural unity of the essay. Such criticism forgets the reason for the architecture, which is to organize and present ideas, with the result that the reader is left with a fascinating scaffolding that supports nothing, thus ignoring what Péguy has really said.

Such criticism renders the enormous task of establishing a genuinely critical and truly complete edition of Péguy's works all the more pressing. The need is great[3] since scholars have not hesitated to list Péguy along with Proust, Gide, and Colette as one of "the truly great prose writers" of the pre-World War I era in France[4] or to claim that he is, along with his contemporaries Proust, Claudel, Gide, and Valéry, "one of the greatest writers of the century."[5] Sustained critical endeavors to demonstrate that greatness have encountered serious obstacles.

The first obstacle was and remains Péguy's style. He was indeed one of "those sowers of ideas"[6] and a great one, but his reader has a difficult time separating the seminal idea from the verbiage that all but drowns it, that is, if he has not already been alienated by a sort of suffocating religiosity that suffuses much of the poetry and the unrelenting violence of many of

the essays. The reader recognizes immediately in Péguy's vigorous and earthy, sometimes hearty and even homely polemics
"one of the least organized, the least Racinian of Frenchmen,
but one of the most authentic sons of the people and of the soil
of France."[7] The voice of that son of the people and of the soil
had been corrupted, however, as one of the great analysts of
style has shown. He noted more than fifty years ago that "Péguy's
style was the necessary consequence of his moral attitude, . . . a
conflict betwen popular inspiration and scholarly inspiration
resulting from his education, between his naive mysticism and
a controlled intellectualism, between his will to live [*vouloir-
vivre*], his desire for animation, for realization, and his quest
for the truth, for discrimination, and for abstraction, between
his poetic temperament and that of the polemicist."[8] As a result,
"Péguy does not attain with his language the purity, as it were,
obvious, polished, and effortless of the mystic sentiment—his
turn of phrase is, for [the expression of] that [sentiment], too
erudite, too reasonable" (p. 125). A later critic has pointed out
that Péguy's prose would never satisfy "the great mass of readers
who continue to consider Voltaire and Chateaubriand as unsur-
passable models." As for his poetry, "it is neither sufficiently
shocking, nor sufficiently hermetic to excite the interest of so-
called advanced critics, but it is a great deal too innovative
to receive the unreserved approval of traditionalists."[9] Because
of the semingly endless convolutions of his style and his verbosity,
Péguy has been accused of obscurity. A scholar has pointed out
that he "never is; on the contrary, his endless repetitions and
illustrations of the obvious are the greatest flaw in his writings."[10]
If "Many pages by Péguy have become obscure" it is only
"because they treated questions that are dead today."[11]

   With that observation we have passed from style to subject
matter in these essays. Why are the issues dead today? One critic
would reply, "However legitimate his anger may have been in
many respects, it must be said nevertheless that Péguy did not
understand his epoch, nor modern thought" because "he was
not sufficiently a psychologist, not sufficiently detached from his
personal, obsessive, almost theological point of view of the
classical man or the ancient man in order to have a taste for
the crisis of contemporary consciousness."[12] He knew nothing of

what was being done in poetry, the theater, the novel, nothing of the "inventive fertility" (p. 195) that completely surrounded him in his dreary "modern" world. That he really knew about it but "chose to ignore it" is hardly a virtue. The judgment of one of Péguy's best commentators where his essay "L'Argent" is concerned could stand for the majority of the essays: "all that amuses for an instant, sometimes moves, most often disconcerts and fatigues. All those 'great men' . . . are so small today! This family quarrel, this display of dirty linen, finally creates disgust, irritation, sometimes even boredom."[13]

Everyone can agree that Péguy was "a commentator, an apologist in poetry and in prose, a polemicist, a celebrator and a reorganizer of the world, a moralist in all ways and all dimensions. But not an inventor. Not a story-teller."[14] The only story Péguy tells is that of Joan of Arc and of course the outlines of this tale were already pretty well fixed. If Péguy's style presents a high hurdle for today's reader, if the men and the events recounted in his essays are pretty much dead issues, if his poetry cannot really be called great except in instances so limited and so isolated as to belie the very term "great," what remains? We have to conclude with Péguy's French critics that he "is a unique man of letters, an unclassifiable writer,"[15] "his work an unclassifiable phenomenon,"[16] and that his genius is "to force admiration in his very faults" (p. 218). Another current of criticism insists that "Péguy, as time goes by, responds more and more to the preoccupations and spiritual needs of our time."[17] We can only hope that it will not again be the preoccupations and needs that led a Robert Brasillach "to regard Péguy as a French national socialist."[18]

Foreigners have even greater difficulty arriving at an impression let alone a judgment of Péguy. One observer who participated in the 1973 centennial celebration of Péguy's birth had this to say:

For me the sad conclusion is that Péguy should have been left in the relative obscurity into which he had gradually slid in the decades after his heroic death in battle in 1914. He was certainly a fine man and an estimable talent, but his wooly socialism, his unorthodox religiosity, and his mystical patriotism all belong hopelessly to the

period between the Dreyfus affair and Sarajevo. So does most of his
verse, composed in astonishing obliviousness to developments in
French poetry from Baudelaire to Mallarmé.[19]

Foreigners do not understand the peculiar appeal of Péguy's
"wooly socialism" for the Frenchman. Yet Péguy's highly indi-
vidualistic concept that included a total refusal to collaborate
let alone cooperate with others in the political arena where unity
is the essential for success, is exactly the type of socialism that
could appeal to the French. Any utopian ideal promoted with
fervor, containing within itself its own implicit defeat, profoundly satisfies the Frenchman's innate distrust of politics
while giving him the opportunity to expatiate at length on what
is undeniably attractive and basically desirable.

Péguy's "unorthodox religiosity" holds an even greater appeal
for the French. Any man who can demonstrate and even prove
by everything he says and does that he is more deeply religious
than almost anyone within the established church, and who
can maintain a firm faith untainted by institutions not only out-
side the establishment but also frequently in spite of and
against it, has most Frenchmen's undying admiration. France may
still pride herself on being the Eldest Daughter of the Church
but the fact is that Catholicism never completely recovered
its place in the Frenchman's heart after the blows dealt religion by the Revolution. Nevertheless, the shining armor of
unshakable faith still exerts its attraction for those who are only
rationally religious or even religiously rational.

Joan of Arc continues to symbolize all that is best and worst
for France both in victory and defeat. With her inspired help
France became a nation but only with the aid of "voices" that
everyone might secretly like to be privileged to hear but whose
existence most rational Frenchmen would want to deny. At every
moment she is still capable of rallying the French spirit to a
cause. That the cause is frequently an outmoded nationalism,
few if any countries can afford today, is beclouded precisely
by the "mystical patriotism" of a Péguy which arouses French
hearts and souls while at the same time deceiving their minds

The content of Péguy's poetry may remain "oblivious" to the
most obvious realities and its form "oblivious" to the develop-

ments in French poetry over the preceding fifty years, yet the majestic cadances of the alexandrine offer a music to the French ear few foreigners can appreciate. Like waves washing ceaselessly over the sand or the gentle winds blowing over the fields of grain of the Beauce, the alexandrine reassures the French with its lulling rhythms and total predictability, particularly after the jarring dislocations and the frequently willed and often willful obscurity practiced by the Symbolists, Dadaists, Surrealists, and their prolific heirs.

As a result, I am convinced that Péguy's ideas may prove more and more outmoded while some of his poetry may continue to occupy a place in the hearts of the sensitive French. They may well consider it a sort of eternal flame, the symbol of history and country and patriotism and resurrection through death. With the passage of time the flame may flicker, but when needed it will no doubt burn brightly again.

Notes and References

To conserve space, references to the Pléiade edition of the *Œuvres poétiques complètes* are indicated by *OP*, to the *Œuvres en prose 1898–1908* by *O* I, and to the *Œuvres en prose 1909–1914* by *O* II. Complete references are given only for those works not included in the bibliography. For works in the bibliography, sufficient information is given to identify them there. All translations are the present author's unless otherwise indicated.

Chapter One

1. *O* I, pp. 1217–47.
2. *OP*, p. 330.

Chapter Two

1. *O* I, pp. 1–8. All further references to this edition will be indicated in parentheses.
2. Secrétain, *Péguy soldat*, p. 68.

Chapter Three

1. *O* I, pp. 561–97. All further references in parentheses in the text are to this edition.
2. Lewis, *Prisoners of Honor*, p. 311.
3. Jussem-Wilson, *Péguy*, p. 41.
4. Secrétain, *Péguy aujord'hui*, p. 347.
5. Jussem-Wilson, *Péguy*, p. 54.
6. Marcel Proust, *La Prisonnière*, vol. 2 (Gallimard, 1923 [1947]), pp. 42–3.

Chapter Four

1. *O* II, pp. 3–51. All further references to this edition will be indicated in parentheses.
2. Halévy, *Péguy*, p. 138.
3. Guyon, *Péguy*, pp. 169–70.
4. Halévy, *Péguy*, p. 297.

Chapter Five

1. *O* II, pp. 843–55. All further references to this edition will be indicated in parentheses.
2. Guyon, *Péguy*, p. 175.
3. Marcel Proust, *Le Temps retrouvé*, vol. 2 (Gallimard, 1927 [1947]), p. 51.
4. Rolland, *Péguy*, II, p. 163.
5. A whole book has been written on the complicated subject of Péguy and Bergson: Henry, *Bergson maître de Péguy*. See also: Bastaire, *Péguy l'insurgé*, pp. 177–80; Jussem-Wilson, *Charles Péguy*, pp. 67–75; Pilkington, *Bergson and His Influence*, pp. 27–98; Quoniam, *La Pensée de Péguy*, pp. 125–29; Rolland, *Péguy*, I, pp. 25–41, II, pp. 139–73; Rousseaux, *Le Prophète Péguy*, I, pp. 35–40; Secrétain, *Péguy soldat de la vérité*, pp. 128–37; Thibaudet and Spitzer in Simone Fraisse, ed., *Les critiques de notre temps et Péguy*, pp. 31–40, 116–25; Viard, *Philosophie de l'art littéraire et socialisme selon Péguy*, pp. 263–72.

Chapter Six

1. *OP*, pp. 23–326. All further references to this edition will be indicated in parentheses.
2. Bastaire, *Péguy*, p. 9.
3. Secrétain, *Péguy soldat de la vérité*, p. 80.
4. Jules Michelet, Chapter III, "La Pucelle d'Orléans, 1429," Chapter IV, "Le Cardinal de Winchester.—Procès et mort de la Pucelle, 1429–1431," in *Histoire de France*, vol. 5 (Hachette, 1841), published separately as *Jeanne d'Arc* (Hachette, 1853).
5. Henri Wallon, *Jeanne d'Arc* (Hachette, 1860).
6. Jules Quicherat, *Procès de condamnation et de réhabilitation de Jeanne d'Arc, dite la Pucelle*, published for the first time according to the manuscripts of the Bibliothèque Nationale (Paris: Renouard, 1841–1849), 5 vols. *Aperçus nouveaux sur l'histoire de Jeanne d'Arc* (Paris: Renouard, 1850).
7. Guyon, *Péguy*, p. 57.
8. Jussem-Wilson, *Péguy*, p. 82.
9. Guyon, *Péguy*, p. 56.
10. Secrétain, *Péguy soldat de la vérité*, p. 218.
11. Dennery et al., *Péguy*, pp. 146, 148.
12. Guyon, *Péguy*, p. 225.

Chapter Seven

1. *OP*, pp. 889–924. All further references to this edition will be indicated in parentheses.

2. Guyon, *Péguy*, p. 231.

3. Secrétain, *Péguy soldat de la vérité*, p. 232.

4. *O II*, p. 30.

5. Halévy, *Péguy*, p. 246.

6. Michel Butor, "Le livre comme objet," *Répertoire II* (Paris: Editions de Minuit, 1964), pp. 7–26.

7. Péguy, *La Ballade de coeur*.

Chapter Eight

1. *O I*, p. 192.

2. *OP*, pp. 93–4.

3. Maurice Schumann, "Sur la mort de Péguy," p. 265.

Chapter Nine

1. Gilbert Zoppi, "Péguy et Molière."

2. Françoise Gerbod, "Polyeucte dans l'oeuvre de Péguy."

3. Henri Peyre, *Qu'est-ce que le classicisme?* (Paris: Nizet, 1965), p. 256.

4. Françoise Gerbod, "La critique littéraire de Péguy appliquée à Corneille."

5. François Desplanques, "Péguy et Hugo ou le critique amoureux."

6. Pierre Albouy, "Péguy et Hugo."

7. Simone Fraisse, "Péguy et Renan."

8. Jean-François Revel, *On Proust*, Trans. Martin Turnell (New York: Library Press, 1972), p. 174.

Chapter Ten

1. Rolland, *Péguy*, vol. 2, p. 263.

2. Viard, *Philosophie de l'art littéraire et socialisme selon Péguy*, p. 374.

3. Jean Bastaire, "Etat présent des études péguystes."

4. Henry Peyre, *Writers and Their Critics* (Ithaca: Cornell University Press, 1944), p. 117.

5. Secrétain, *Péguy aujourd'hui*, p. 291.

6. Henri Peyre, *Les Générations littéraires* (Boivin, 1948), p. 38.

7. Henri Peyre, *Qu'est-ce que le classicisme?* (Nizet, 1965), p. 262.

8. Léo Spitzer, "L'elan vital," in Simone Fraisse, ed., *Les critiques de notre temps et Péguy*, p. 124.

9. Guyon, *Péguy*, p. 279.

10. Peyre, *Writers and Their Critics*, p. 198.
11. Guyon, *Péguy*, p. 239.
12. Secrétain, *Péguy soldat de la vérité*, pp. 194–5.
13. Guyon, *Péguy,* p. 239.
14. Secrétain, *Péguy soldat de la vérité*, p. 211.
15. Guyon, *Péguy*, p. 281.
16. Secrétain, *Péguy soldat de la vérité*, p. 211.
17. Quoniam, *La Pensée de Péguy*, p. 19.
18. William R. Tucker, *The Fascist Ego: A Political Biography of Robert Brasillach* (Berkeley: University of California Press, 1975), p. 44.
19. Roy McMullen, "Foreign Post: Two Literary Letters: Paris," *World*, no. 7 (March 27, 1973), p. 54.

Selected Bibliography

The Péguy bibliography is growing rapidly. I have included those items, new and old, that I found most useful. The place of publication is Paris unless otherwise indicated.

PRIMARY SOURCES

1. Poetry, Plays, and Prose.

L'Argent, followed by *L'Argent suite.* Gallimard, 1932.
La Ballade du coeur, unpublished poem by Charles Péguy. Edited and introduced by Julie Sabiani. Klincksieck, 1973.
Le Mystère de la charité de Jeanne d'Arc, with two unpublished acts. Edition established according to the manuscripts by Albert Béguin with the help of Mrs. Charles Péguy and Mr. Alfred Saffrey. Le Club du meilleur livre, 1956.
Le Mystère des Saints Innocents, Collection Soleil. Gallimard, 1929.
Notre Patrie. Gallimard, 1915.
Œuvres complètes, 20 vols. Gallimard, 1916–1955. [Incomplete but republished by Slatkine in 1974.]
Œuvres en prose (1898–1908). Introduction and Notes by Marcel Péguy, Bibliothèque de la Pléiade 140. Gallimard, 1959. [Reprinted in 1965.]
Œuvres en prose (1909–1914). Foreword, Chronology, Notes, Bibliography, and Index by Marcel Péguy, Bibliothèque de la Pléiade 122. Gallimard, 1961. [Reprinted in 1968.]
Œuvres poétiques complètes. Introduction by François Porché. Chronology of the life and works by Pierre Péguy, Notes by Marcel Péguy, Bibliothèque de la Pléiade 60. Gallimard, 1957. [Reprinted in 1967.]
Les Œuvres posthumes de Charles Péguy. Edited by Jacques Viard. Minard, 1969.
Péguy tel qu'on l'ignore, Texts selected and introduced by Jean Bastaire, Collection Idées 291. Gallimard, 1973. [Twenty-six brief excerpts from works not published in the Pléiade editions.]
Prières. Edited by Paul Doncoeur. Gallimard, 1934.

157

2. Correspondence

Lettres à André Bourgeois. L'Amitié Charles Péguy, 1950.
Lettres et entretiens. Edited by Marcel Péguy. Artisan du Livre, 1927.
Alain-Fournier, Charles Péguy, Correspondence 1910–1914. Intro-
    duction and Notes by Yves Rey-Herme. Fayard, 1973.
Pour l'Honneur de l'esprit. Correspondence between Charles Péguy
    and Romain Rolland, 1898–1914. Introduction and Notes by
    Auguste Martin, Cahiers Romain Rolland. Albin Michel, 1973.

3. Translations

Basic Verities, Prose and Poetry. Translated by Ann and Julien
    Green. New York: Pantheon, 1943.
God Speaks, Religious Poetry. Translation and Introduction by Julien
    Green. New York: Pantheon, 1945.
Men and Saints, Prose and Poetry. Translated by Ann and Julien
    Green. New York: Pantheon, 1944.
The Mystery of the Charity of Joan of Arc. Translated by Julien
    Green. New York: Pantheon, 1950.
The Portico of the Mystery of the Second Virtue. Translated by Doro-
    thy Brown Aspinwall. Metuchen, New Jersey: Scarecrow Press,
    1970.

4. Periodicals

Cahiers de la Quinzaine, Fifteen Series, 1900–1914. [The entire
    series, including the "Precursors" (1897–1899), is being re-
    printed by Slatkine in Geneva beginning in 1974.]
Cahiers de l'Amitié Charles Péguy. No. 1 (November, 1947) through
    the final issue, No. 25 (1972).
Carnet Péguy 1965, 1966, etc., published annually by the *Cahiers de
    l'Amitié Charles Péguy.*
Feuillets de l'Amitié Charles Péguy. No. 1 (August 28, 1948) through
    No. 208 (April, 1976). [Still appearing.]

SECONDARY SOURCES

1. Books

BASTAIRE, JEAN. *Péguy l'insurgé*, Collection Traces. Payon, 1975.
    Balanced review of Péguy's thought and philosophy.
CHAPMAN, GUY. *The Dreyfus Case, A Reassessment.* New York:
    Reynal, 1955. Clear and well documented history of a compli-
    cated affair.

CHRISTOPHE, LUCIEN. *Le Jeune Homme Péguy, de la source au fleuve* (*1897–1905*), Collection La Lettre et L'Esprit. Louvière: Renaissance du livre, 1964. A careful review of Péguy's evolution from 1897 to 1905 as seen in his published and unpublished works.

COURSAGET, JEAN. *Péguy et Chartres*, Exposition for the centenary of his birth. Luisant: Durand, 1973. Useful little catalogue.

DENNERY, ETIENNE; Hubert, Marie-Clotilde; and Brunet, Michel. *Charles Péguy*. Bibliothèque Nationale, 1974. Catalogue of the Centennial exhibition containing many useful facts.

FRAISSE, SIMONE. *Péguy et le monde antique*. Armand Colin, 1973. A detailed history of the influences that formed Péguy's classical spirit and their effects on his works.

————, ed. *Les Critiques de notre temps et Péguy*. Garnier, 1973. Informative essays by everyone from Péguy's contemporaries to the "New" critics. Useful bibliography.

GUYON, BERNARD. *Péguy*, Connaissance des lettres 55. Hatier, 1960. After more than fifteen years still one of the best books on *Péguy*.

HALÉVY, DANIEL. *Péguy and "Les Cahiers de la Quinzaine."* Translated by Ruth Bethell. New York: Longmans, Green, 1947. Important biography by a contemporary of Péguy.

HENRY, ANDRÉ. *Bergson maître de Péguy*. Les Jeunes Etudes Philosophiques. Elzévir, 1948. A thoughtful analysis of this complicated relationship.

JOHANNET, RENÉ. *Vie et mort de Péguy*. Flammarion, 1950. The author, who knew Péguy, has written a detailed biography with some appreciation of the works.

JUSSEM-WILSON, N(ELLY). *Charles Péguy*. Studies in Modern European Literature and Thought. London: Bowes and Bowes, 1965. A brief but well documented introduction to Péguy.

LEWIS, DAVID L. *Prisoners of Honor: The Dreyfus Affair*. New York: William Morrow, 1973. A more recent and somewhat more impassioned study of the affair.

NELSON, ROY JAY. *Péguy poète du sacré*. Essay on the poetics of Péguy. Minard, 1960. Detailed, very useful analysis of the symbols and images in Péguy's poetics.

PÉGUY, MARCEL. *La Rupture de Charles Péguy et de Georges Sorel* according to unpublished documents. Artisan du Livre, 1930. A careful but not unbiased analysis of the causes of the break between two old friends.

PEYRE, ANDRÉ. *Péguy sans cocarde*. Interview with Roger Secrétain, Preface by Professor Robert Debré, illustrations by Roger

Toulouse. Millas-Martin, 1973. Illuminating conversations on Péguy and his works, but only for those who already know the works.

QUONIAM, THÉODORE. La Pensée de Péguy, Collection Pour Connaître. Bordas, 1967. Clear view of Péguy's thought but without constructive criticism.

Rencontres avec Péguy: Autour d'un centenaire (1873–1973), Acts of the Colloquium in Nice (May 1973). Desclée de Brouwer, 1975. Ten articles on as many aspects of the works of Péguy with several new points of departure. See the "Articles" section of this bibliography.

REY-HERMES, YVES. Péguy, Collection Présence littéraire. Bordas, 1973. Concise evaluation of the thought and works of Péguy.

ROLLAND, ROMAIN. Péguy, 2 vols. Albin Michel, 1944. Reprinted in 1973. Important biography by a contemporary of Péguy.

ROUSSEAUX, ANDRÉ. Le Prophète Péguy (Introduction to the Reading of the Work of Péguy), 2 vols. Albin Richel, 1946. A sensitive, profoundly Christian interpretation of Péguy as Biblical prophet. Lengthy but somewhat limited by its approach.

ROUSSEL, JEAN. Mesure de Péguy. Corrêa, 1946. Personal and uncritical evaluation of Péguy and his works.

————. Charles Péguy. Preface by Daniel Rops, Classiques du XXe siècle. Editions Universitaires, 1952. Brief, general introduction to Péguy's works.

SERVAIS, YVONNE. Charles Péguy: the Pursuit of Salvation. Westminster, Maryland: Newman Press, 1953. A solid sober account of Péguy's life and works up to 1909.

SCHMITT, HANS A. Charles Péguy: The Decline of an Idealist. Baton Rouge: Louisiana State University Press, 1967. Carefully documented account of the evolution of Péguy's thought, negative but honest. Useful bibliography.

SECRÉTAIN, ROGER. Péguy soldat de la vérité followed by Péguy aujourd'hui. Perrin, 1972. The texts are dated 1939 and 1972. The earlier work is far the better but they both contain well balanced judgments.

THARAUD, JÉRÔME ET JEAN. Notre cher Péguy, 2 vols. Plon, 1926. Personal souvenirs important for an understanding of Péguy the man and his time.

————. Pour les fidèles de Péguy. Artisan du Livre, 1927. More personal souvenirs by two of Péguy's contemporaries.

VIARD, JACQUES. Philosophie de l'art littéraire et socialisme selon Péguy (et selon Balzac, Berdiaev, Bernanos, Bernard-Lazare, Hugo, Leroux, Michelet, Proudhon, Proust, Simone Weil, etc. . .). Bibliothèque Française et Romane, Serie C: Etudes littéraires XIX. Klincksieck, 1969. One of the most important recent books on Péguy but almost impossible to read.

VIGNEAULT, ROBERT. *L'univers féminin dans l'oeuvre de Charles Péguy.* Essay on the creative imagination of a poet, Essais pour notre temps 6. Desclée de Brouwer, 1967. The preponderant role of women in Péguy's works analyzed from a literary point of view.

VILLIERS, MARJORIE. *Charles Péguy: A Study in Integrity.* New York: Harper & Row, 1965. The best biographical introduction to Péguy in English.

2. Articles

ABRAHAM, MARCEL. "Enfance de Charles Péguy," *Le Mail,* no. xii (Spring, 1929), pp. 1–7.

————. "Les devoirs de Péguy," *Le Mail,* no. xii (Spring, 1929), pp. 16–18.

ALBOUY, PIERRE. "Péguy et Hugo," *Revue d'histoire littéraire de la France,* no. 2–3 (March-June 1973), pp. 254–63.

ANTOINE, GÉRALD. "Jalons pour une étude stylistique de Péguy," in *Péguy, Actes du Colloque international d'Orléans* (Minard, 1966), pp. 327–35.

————. "La Joie des mots chez Péguy," *Revue d'histoire littéraire de la France,* no. 2–3 (March-June 1973), pp. 516–36.

————. "Le thème de l'enfance chez Péguy," in *Rencontres avec Péguy,* pp. 55–78.

Australian Journal of French Studies: Charles Péguy et la critique littéraire, no. 1 (1973), pp. 11–108.

AVRIL, YVES. "Exigence et acceptation," *Esprit,* no. 330 (August-September 1964), pp. 407–10.

BALIBAR, RENÉE. "Sur le personnage de Madame Gervaise dans Péguy," *Revue d'histoire littéraire de la France,* no. 2–3 (March-June 1973), pp. 225–36.

————. "Le conflit des écritures" in Simone Fraisse, ed., *Les critiques de notre temps et Péguy,* pp. 159–70.

BALTHASAR, HANS URS VON. "Les métamorphoses de l'enfer," *Esprit,* no. 330 (August-September 1964), pp. 288–316.

BARBÉRIS, PIERRE. "La notion de peuple chez Péguy," *Péguy, Actes du Colloque international d'Orléans* (Minard, 1966), pp. 78–91.

————. "Peuple et prolétariat" in Simone Fraisse, ed., *Les critiques de notre temps et Péguy,* pp. 170–77.

BARNES, ANNIE. "Péguy et Molière," in W. D. Howarth and Merlin

Thomas, eds., *Molière: Stage and Study*, Essays in Honour of
W. G. Moore (Oxford: Cladendon Press, 1973), pp. 218–37.

BARRÈS, MAURICE. "Jeanne d'Arc" in Simone Fraisse, ed., *Les critiques de notre temps et Péguy*, pp. 49–53.

BARTENSTEIN, WINFRED. "Un lecteur allemand," *Esprit*, no. 330
(August-September 1964), pp. 421–28.

BASTAIRE, JEAN. "Le fidèle Péguy," *Esprit*, no. 330 (August-September
1964), pp. 396–406.

————. "Le patriotisme de Péguy avant 1950," *Péguy, Actes du Colloque international d'Orléans* (Minard, 1966), pp. 92–108.

————. "Péguy et le réalisme poétique d'Alain-Fournier," *Australian Journal of French Studies*, no. 1 (January-April 1973), pp. 79–90.

————. "Péguy prophète de la liberté socialiste," *Etudes*, February 1973, pp. 245–61.

————. "Etat présent des études péguystes," *Revue d'histoire littéraire de la France*, no. 2–3 (March-June 1973), pp. 195–205.

————. "Péguy l'insurgé," *La Nouvelle Revue Française*, no. 244 (April 1973), pp. 58–65.

————. "Les Cahiers de la Quinzaine," *Revue des Deux Mondes*, no. 7 (July 1973), pp. 65–72.

————. "Péguy et les Milliet," in *Littérature et société: Recueil d'études en l'honneur de Bernard Guyon* (Desclée de Brouwer, 1973), pp. 149–60.

BÉGUIN, ALBERT. "Actualité de Péguy, *Esprit*, no. 330 (August-September 1964), pp. 388–95.

————. "Le monde antique" in Simone Fraisse, ed., *Les critiques de notre temps et Péguy*, pp. 64–71.

————. "L'Incarnation" in Simone Fraisse, ed., *Les critiques de notre temps et Péguy*, pp. 81–86.

BENDA, JULIEN. "Lettre," *Le Mail*, no. xxi (Spring, 1929), p. 49.

BERNANOS, GEORGES. "Son heure sonnera...," *Esprit*, no. 330 (August-September 1964), pp. 437–41.

BIRNBERG, JACQUES. "Le socialisme intégral," *Espirit*, no. 330 (August-September 1964), pp. 343–57.

BLANCHET, CHARLES. "Péguy et Ramuz," *Esprit*, no. 330 (August-September 1964), pp. 379–87.

BONNAUD-LAMOTTE, D. "Péguy, poète et témoin de la Commune," *Pensée*, no. 164 (August 1972), pp. 79–98.

————. "Péguy éditeur des 'Cahiers rouges,'" *Revue d'histoire littéraire de la France*, no. 2–3 (March-June 1973), pp. 417–26.

————. "Les Russes et la Russie des années 1900 dans les 'Cahiers de la Quinzaine,'" in *Littérature et société: Recueil d'études en l'honneur de Bernard Guyon* (Desclée de Brouwer, 1973), pp. 161–72.

BURAC, ROBERT. "L'Ennemi de l'intérieur, Sur une structure de Péguy," *Revue d'histoire littéraire de la France*, no. 2–3 (March-June 1973), pp. 427–40.

CAHM, ERIC. "Péguy et sa politique vus d'Angleterre," *Esprit*, no. 330 (August-September 1964), pp. 411–20.

————. "Fidélité de Péguy à la tradition socialiste," *Péguy, Actes du Colloque international d'Orléans* (Minard, 1966), pp. 58–77.

CHABANON, ALBERT. "Les deux rythmiques" in Simone Fraisse, ed., *Les critiques de notre temps et Péguy*, pp. 132–35.

CHABOT, JACQUES. "Bernanos et Péguy" in Max Milner, ed., *Bernanos* (Plon, 1972), pp. 465–79.

CHRISTOPHE, LUCIEN. "Ferveur et fraternité," *Péguy, Actes du Colloque international d'Orléans* (Minard, 1966), pp. 231–34.

COPEAU, JACQUES. "Introduction à une lecture," *Le Mail*, no. xii (Spring, 1929), pp. 43–45.

————. "Lettres de Jaques Copeau à Charles Péguy," *La Nouvelle Revue Française*, no. 244 (April 1973), pp. 89–92.

DANIÉLOU, JEAN CARDINAL. "Actualité de Péguy," *Revue des Deux Mondes*, no. 10 (October 1973), pp. 36–46.

————. "Péguy et les Pères de l'Eglise," in *Littérature et société: Recueil d'études en l'honneur de Bernard Guyon* (Desclée de Brouwer, 1973), pp. 173–79.

DEBRÉ, ROBERT, "Charles Péguy: Pages de souvenirs," *Revue des Deux Mondes*, no. 5 (May 1973), pp. 299–305.

DELAPORTE, JEAN, "L'expérience spirituelle de Péguy," *Péguy, Actes du Colloque international d'Orléans* (Minard, 1966), pp. 213–30.

————. "Péguy et le socialisme scientifique (correspondance avec l'économiste Walras)," *Esprit*, no. 365 (January 1967), pp. 93–99.

————. "Péguy et le Catholicisme français au début du siècle," *La Table Ronde*, no. 229 (February 1967), pp. 43–59.

DENT, A., "Péguy et le retour au texte," *Australian Journal of French Studies*, no. 1 (January-April 1973), pp. 91–93.

DESPLANQUES, FRANÇOIS, "Le corps, la parole et le jeu dans la démarche critique de Péguy," *Australian Journal of French Studies*, no. 1 (January-April 1973), pp. 102–08.

————. "Péguy, lecteur de la Passion," *Revue d'histoire littéraire de la France*, no. 2–3 (March-June 1973), pp. 449–58.

————. "Péguy et Hugo ou le critique amoureux," in *Rencontres avec Péguy*, pp. 177–84.

DEVAUX, ANDRÉ-A., "D'un malentendu entre Péguy et Bergson,"

Revue d'histoire littéraire de la France, no. 2–3 (March-June 1973), pp. 281–99.

————. "Réalité et vérité selon Charles Péguy," in *Rencontres avec Péguy*, pp. 81–118.

DORGELÈS, ROLAND. "Témoignage," *Le Mail*, no. xii (Spring, 1929), pp. 38–39.

DUPLOYÉ, PIE. "Les 'curés,'" *Esprit*, no. 330 (August-September 1964), pp. 264–87.

————. "L'Europe culturelle" in Simone Fraisse, ed., *Les critiques de notre temps et Péguy*, pp. 59–64.

————. "La Mélancolie virgilienne," *Revue d'histoire littéraire de la France*, no. 2–3 (March-June 1973), pp. 459–69.

EMMANUEL, PIERRE. "Le serviteur du Verbe incarné," *Esprit*, no. 330 (August-September 1964), pp. 358–73.

————. "Péguy serviteur du verbe incarné," in *Le monde est intérieur* (Seuil, 1967), pp. 185–205.

ESPIAU DE LA MAESTRE, ANDRÉ. "La pénétration de Péguy en Allemagne de 1910 à nos jours," *Péguy, Actes du Colloque international d'Orléans* (Minard, 1966), pp. 348–61.

Esprit: Péguy reconnu, no. 330 (August-September 1964), pp. 196–441.

FAVRE, YVES-ALAIN. "Poesie et liturgie dans les trois 'Mystères' de Péguy," *Revue d'histoire littéraire de la France*, no. 2–3 (March-June 1973), pp. 441–48.

FÉRET, H.-M. "Péguy, les 'curés' et la croix de Jésus," *Péguy, Actes du Colloque international d'Orléans* (Minard, 1966), pp. 276–98.

FRAISSE, SIMONE. "Péguy et le monde antique," *Esprit*, no. 330 (August-September 1964), pp. 317–30.

————. "Le monde antique dans la religion de Péguy." *Péguy, Actes du Colloque international d'Orléans* (Minard, 1966), pp. 188–92.

————. "Péguy et la Sorbonne," *Revue d'histoire littéraire de la France*, no. 3 (May-June 1970), pp. 416–34.

————. "Le texte et la glose," *Australian Journal of French Studies*, no. 1 (January-April 1973), pp. 94–101.

————. "Péguy et Renan," *Revue d'histoire littéraire de la France*, no. 2–3 (March-June 1973), pp. 264–80.

————. "L'ambivalence du thème de la route dans *Eve* et *Suite d'Eve*," in *Recontres avec Péguy*, pp. 169–73.

————. "Péguy, Lanson et le lansonisme," in *Littérature et société: Recueil d'études en l'honneur de Benard Guyon* (Desclée de Brouwer, 1973), pp. 181–90.

FRANCIS, RAYMOND. "L'Humour de Péguy," *Revue d'histoire littéraire de la France*, no. 2–3 (March-June 1973), pp. 504–15.

FRITZ, GÉRARD. "La Réflexion de Péguy sur le langage et son style," *Revue d'histoire littéraire de la France,* no. 2–3 (March-June 1973), pp. 491–503.

FUMET, STANISLAS. "Souvenirs," *Le Mail,* no. xii (Spring, 1929), p. 32–37.

GARRIE, ROBERT. "Peuple de Paris...," *Le Mail,* no. xii (Spring, 1929), pp. 72–75.

GAULMIER, JEAN. "Péguy, prophète romantique," *Péguy, Actes du Colloque international d'Orléans* (Minard, 1966), pp. 300–03.

GÉNEVOIX, MAURICE. "Lettre," *Le Mail,* no. xii (Spring, 1929), pp. 41–42.

GERBOD, FRANÇOISE. "La critique littéraire de Péguy appliquée à Corneille," *Australian Journal of French Studies,* no. 1 (January-April 1973), pp. 11–32.

————. "La figure de Polyeucte dans l'oeuvre de Péguy," *Revue d'histoire littéraire de la France,* no. 2–3 (March-June 1973), pp. 237–53.

GIDE, ANDRÉ "La flûte arabe" in Simone Fraisse, ed., *Les critiques de notre temps et Péguy,* pp. 113–16.

GILLET, LOUIS. "Trios instantanés" in Simone Fraisse, ed., *Les critiques de notre temps et Péguy,* pp. 13–15.

GIORDAN, HENRI. "Contribution à l'histoire des *Cahiers,*" *Péguy, Actes du Colloque international d'Orléans* (Minard, 1966), pp. 336–46.

GRASSET, BERNARD. "Evangile de l'édition selon Péguy," *La Table Ronde,* no. 85 (January 1966), pp. 11–36; no. 86 (February 1966), pp. 64–95.

GUIBERTEAU, PHILIPPE. "Défense et illustration de Charles Péguy," *Le Mail,* no. xii (Spring, 1929), pp. 50–61.

————. "Péguy, Guénon, et les anciens mondes," *Péguy, Actes du Colloque international d'Orléans* (Minard, 1966), pp. 235–44.

————. "Les âmes parallèles de Dante et de Péguy," in *Littérature et société: Recueil d'études en l'honneur de Bernard Guyon* (Desclée de Brouwer, 1973), pp. 197–206.

GUILLEMIN, HENRI. "Péguy et le sixième commandement," in *Précisions* (Gallimard, 1973), pp. 345–76.

————. "A propos du *Péguy* de Romain Rolland" in *Précisions* (Gallimard, 1973), pp. 377–95.

————. "Enfant de lumière ou fils des ténèbres?" in Simone Fraisse, ed., *Les critiques de notre temps et Péguy,* pp. 107–9.

GUY, BASIL. "Notes on Péguy and Antiquity" in Walter G. Langlois, ed., *The Persistent Voice: Essays on Hellenism in French Literature since the 18th Century in Honor of Professor Henri M.*

Peyre (New York: New York University Press, 1971), pp. 93–108.

GUYON, BERNARD. "Fidélités ou reniements," *Péguy, Actes du Colloque international d'Orléans* (Minard, 1966), pp. 13–24.

—————. "Les Prémices du génie," *Australian Journal of French Studies*, no. 1 (January-April 1973), pp. 42–49.

—————. "Péguy contre l'école?" *Revue d'histoire littéraire de la France*, no. 2–3 (March-June 1973), pp. 206–24.

—————. "Le combat spirituel de Charles Péguy," *Revue des Deux Mondes*, no. 5 (May 1973), pp. 306–28.

—————. "Patrie et mémoire," in Simone Fraisse, ed., *Les critiques de notre temps et Péguy*, pp. 53–59 (Excerpt from *Péguy.*)

GUYOT, CHARLY. "Charles Péguy et la critique protestante," *Péguy, Actes du Colloque international d'Orléans* (Minard, 1966), pp. 245–52.

HALÉVY, DANIEL. "La République," in Simone Fraisse, ed., *Les critiques de notre temps et Péguy*, pp. 72–77. (Excerpt from *Péguy et les Cahiers de la Quinzaine.*)

HARDRÉ, JACQUES. "Charles Péguy et Albert Camus: esquisse d'un parallèle," *The French Review*, no. 4 (February 1967), pp. 471–84.

JENNY, HENRI. "L'album biblique de Péguy," *Péguy, Actes du Colloque international d'Orléans* (Minard, 1966), pp. 193–201.

JONES, GRAHAME C. "Graham Greene and the legend of Péguy," *Comparative Literature*, no. 2 (Spring, 1969), pp. 139–45.

JORDAN, MICHEL. "La rupture de Péguy avec les socialistes," *Péguy, Actes du Colloque international d'Orléans* (Minard, 1966), pp. 145–49.

KURATA, KIYOSHI. "La volonté de Péguy dans sa marche en Beauce," *Péguy, Actes du Colloque international d'Orléans*, (Minard, 1966), pp. 304–09.

LAICHTER, FRANTISEK. "Une rénovation créatrice et militaire," *Esprit*, no. 330 (August-September 1964), pp. 429–36.

—————. "L'actualité de Charles Péguy," *Péguy, Actes du Colloque international d'Orléans* (Minard, 1966), pp. 362–73.

LECOMTE, GUY. "Charles Péguy et l'accueil du réel" in *Littérature et société: Recueil d'études en l'honneur de Bernard Guyon* (Desclée de Brouwer, 1973), pp. 207–20.

—————. "Péguy et le modernisme" in *Recontres avec Péguy*, pp. 31–40.

LE RÉVÉREND, ANDRÉ. "Mystique et politique chez Péguy et Lyautey" in *Littérature et société: Recueil d'études en l'honneur de Bernard Guyon* (Desclée de Brouwer, 1973), pp. 221–29.

LEROY, GÉRALDI. "Péguy et l'économie mathématique," *Revue d'histoire littéraire de la France*, no. 2–3 (March-June 1973), pp. 395–406.

————. "Les fondements anarchistes de la pensée politique de Charles Péguy" in *Littérature et société: Recueil d'études en l'honneur de Bernard Guyon* (Desclée de Brouwer, 1973), pp. 231–43.

————. "L'institution des Cahiers de la Quinzaine, 1900," in *Rencontres avec Péguy*, pp. 17–30.

Le Mail, Cahiers Trimestriels de Littérature: Charles Péguy, poète de Jeanne d'Arc, no. xxi (Spring, 1929), 103pp.

MAMBRINO, JEAN. "Charles Péguy, poète et socialiste," *Etudes*, August-September 1970, pp. 222–36.

MARCHAND, JACQUELINE. "Péguy et Paul Bondois: lettres inédites," *Revue d'histoire littéraire de la France*, no. 2–3 (March-June 1973), pp. 300–25.

MARTIN, AUGUSTE. "Bilan des études sur Péguy," *Péguy, Actes du Colloque international d'Orléans* (Minard, 1966), pp. 313–26.

————. "Le dossier Bergson-Péguy," *Les études bergsoniennes, Tome VIII* (Presses Universitaires de France, 1968), pp. 3–12.

MARTIN DU GARD, MAURICE. "Barrès et Péguy sous l'occupation" in *Les libéraux de Renan à Chardonne* (Plon, 1967), pp. 105–09.

MASSIS, HENRI. "Péguy et nous," in *Au long d'une vie* (Plon, 1967), pp. 63–72.

————. "Cinquante ans après: Présence de Péguy," in *Au long d'une vie* (Plon, 1967), pp. 78–84.

MELCHIOR-BRUNET, ALAIN. "L'itinéraire de Charles Péguy," *Vie et langage*, no. 250 (January 1973), pp. 9–15.

MONTHERLANT, HENRY DE. "Hommage," *Le Mail*, no. xii (Spring, 1929), p. 40.

MOUNIER, EMMANUEL. "Pour une philosophie engagée" in Simone Fraisse, ed., *Les critiques de notre temps et Péguy*, pp. 23–31.

NELSON, ROY JAY. "La notion de fidélité dans l'oeuvre de Péguy," *Péguy, Actes du Colloque international d'Orléans* (Minard, 1966), pp. 25–35.

La Nouvelle Revue Française: Charles Péguy, no. 244 (April 1973), pp. 58–96.

OLIVIER, R. "Notes sur le mot 'moderne' chez Péguy," *Le Français Moderne*, no. 2 (April 1969), pp. 148–59; no. 3 (July 1969), pp. 240–53; no. 4 (October 1969), pp. 317–29.

ONIMUS, JEAN. "La 'prise de chair' chez Péguy," *Etudes*, no. 10 (November 1946), pp. 163–80.

————. "Travaux et recherches concernant Péguy. Suggestions et perspectives d'avenir," *Péguy, Actes du Colloque international d'Orléans* (Minard, 1966), pp. 376–83.

————. "Connaissance de Péguy" in Charles B. Osburn, ed., *The Present State of French Studies: A Collection of Research Reviews* (Metuchen, New Jersey: Scarecrow Press, 1971), pp. 808–24.

————. "Péguy, la différence et la répétition," *Revue d'histoire littéraire de la France,* no. 2–3 (March-June 1973), pp. 470–90.

————. "Images de vie, images de mort" in Simone Fraisse, ed., *Les critiques de notre temps et Péguy,* pp. 136–45.

————. "Actualité de Péguy" in *Rencontres avec Péguy,* pp. 11–14.

PARENT, MONIQUE. "La phrase poétique" in Simone Fraisse, ed., *Les critiques de notre temps et Péguy,* pp. 125–32.

PÉGUY, MARCEL. "Les pèlerinages de Charles Péguy," *Le Mail,* no. xii (Spring 1929), pp. 76–83.

————. "Le Lieutenant Péguy, soldat de France," *Revue d'histoire littéraire de la France,* no. 2–3 (March-June 1973), pp. 381–94.

PESLOÜAN, CHARLES LUCAS DE. "Lettre," *Le Mail,* no. xii (Spring, 1929), pp. 24–29.

PILKINGTON, A. E. "Charles Péguy" in *Bergson and His Influence, A Reassessment* (Cambridge: Cambridge University Press, 1976), pp. 27–98.

QUONIAM, THÉO. "La prière de Péguy. Foi philosophique et foi religieuse," *Péguy, Actes du Colloque international d'Orléans* (Minard, 1966), pp. 107–12.

RABI. "Israël," *Esprit,* no. 330 (August-September 1964), pp. 331–42.

————. "Charles Péguy et Blanche Raphaël," *Nouveaux Cahiers,* no. 22 (Autumn, 1970), pp. 28–31.

Revue d'histoire littéraire de la France: Péguy, no. 2–3 (March-June 1973), pp. 193–536.

REY-HERME, YVES. "Charles Péguy et Alain-Fournier," *Revue d'histoire littéraire de la France,* no. 2–3 (March-June 1973), pp. 407–16.

ROBINET, ANDRÉ. "Péguy, lecteur de Bergson. Première rencontre," *Les études bergsoniennes,* Tome VIII (Presses Universitaires de France, 1968), pp. 61–81.

————. "Kant et les mains pures" in Simone Fraisse, ed., *Les critiques de notre temps et Péguy,* pp. 40–48.

ROCHE, ANNE. "Péguy et le socialisme scientifique dans les 'Œuvres posthumes.'" *Revue d'histoire littéraire de la France,* no. 2–3 (March-June 1973), pp. 407–16.

————. "Instituteurs et professeurs parmi les abonnés aux Cahiers de la Quinzaine (premières séries)," in *Littérature et société:*

Recueil d'études en l'honneur de Bernard Guyon (Desclée de Brouwer, 1973), pp. 245–57.

————. "Pour une lecture marxiste de Péguy?" in *Rencontres avec Péguy*, pp. 149–58.

ROLLAND, ROMAIN. "Le pamphlétaire" in Simone Fraisse, ed., *Les critiques de notre temps et Péguy*, pp. 87–99. [Excerpt from *Péguy*.]

ROUSSEAUX, ANDRÉ. "La race" in Simone Fraisse, ed., *Les critiques de notre temps et Péguy*, pp. 77–80. [Excerpts from *Le Prophète Péguy*.]

ROUSSELOT, JEAN. "Péguy, poète aujourd'hui," *Vie et langage*, no. 250 (January 1973), pp. 16–24.

SABIANI, JULIE. " 'Coeur dévoré d'amour,' " *La Nouvelle Revue Française*, no. 244 (April 1973), pp. 76–82.

————. " 'Les ressourcements du coeur,' " *Revue des Deux Mondes*, no. 6 (June 1973), pp. 610–16.

————. "Le Sphynx, la licorne et les cyprès," in *Littérature et société: Recueil d'études en l'honneur de Bernard Guyon* (Desclée de Brouwer, 1973), pp. 259–68.

————. "L'âme charnelle, la femme et l'enfant selon G. Sand et Ch. Péguy, Apôtres de l'amour universel," in *Rencontres avec Péguy*, pp. 119–30.

SAFFREY, H.-D. "La conversion de Péguy et la passion selon saint Matthieu," *Péguy, Actes du Colloque international d'Orléans* (Minard, 1966), pp. 272–75.

SCHUMANN, MAURICE. "Sur la mort de Péguy," *Revue des Deux Mondes*, no. 2 (February 1974), pp. 265–81.

SECRÉTAIN, ROGER. "Chartres," *Le Mail*, no. xii (Spring, 1929), pp. 90–96.

————. "L'anarchiste" in Simone Fraisse, ed., *Les critiques de notre temps et Péguy*, pp. 99–106. [Excerpt from *Péguy soldat de la vérité*.]

SPITZER, LÉO. "L'élan vital" in Simone Fraisse, ed., *Les critiques de notre temps et Péguy*, pp. 116–24.

TAYLOR, STANLEY WILLIAM. "Fidélité de Péguy à l'école," *Péguy, Actes du Colloque international d'Orléans* (Minard, 1966), pp. 42–48.

THARAUD, JÉRÔME ET JEAN. "Souvenirs" in Simone Fraisse, ed., *Les critiques de notre temps et Péguy*, pp. 16–22. [Excerpt from *Notre cher Péguy*.]

THIBAUD, PAUL. "L'anti-Jaurès." *Esprit*, no. 330 (August-September 1964), pp. 240–63.

————. "Péguy et Jaurès. La signification de l'opposition à Jaurès."

Péguy, Actes du Colloque international d'Orléans (Minard, 1966), pp. 150–60.

————. "La pensée économique de Péguy" in *Rencontres avec Péguy*, pp. 137–47.

THIBAUDET, ALBERT. "Bergson et la durée" in Simone Fraisse, ed., *Les critiques de notre temps et Péguy*, pp. 31–40.

THISSE, PAUL. "Les Péguysmes que j'ai vécus," *Péguy, Actes du Colloque international d'Orléans* (Minard, 1966), pp. 161–64.

VADÉ, YVES. "Au péril du monde moderne," *Esprit*, no. 330 (August-September 1964), pp. 196–215.

————. "Fidélité de Péguy à l'enfance," *Péguy, Actes du Colloque international d'Orléans* (Minard, 1966), pp. 36–41.

VARILLON, FRANÇOIS. "Charles Péguy: l'ordre et la liberté," *Etudes*, June 1973, pp. 861–78.

VIARD, JACQUES. "Anarchiste," *Esprit*, no. 330 (August-September 1964), pp. 216–39.

————. "Péguy et le communisme d'enseignement," *Péguy, Actes du Colloque international d'Orléans* (Minard, 1966), pp. 109–33.

————. "Peguy et les deux romantismes," *Australian Journal of French Studies*, no. 1 (January-April 1973), pp. 50–78.

————. "Prophètes d'Israël et annonciateur chrétien d'après les archives inédites des 'Cahiers,'" *Revue d'histoire littéraire de la France*, no. 2–3 (March-June 1973), pp. 333–80.

————. "Péguy et Proust ou la foi dans les Lettres," *La Nouvelle Revue Française*, no. 244 (April 1973), pp. 66–75.

————. "Un nouveau Jean-Jacques" in Simone Fraisse, ed., *Les critiques de notre temps et Péguy*, pp. 109–12.

————. "Péguy et les religieux républicains de 'L'Encyclopédie Nouvelle'" in *Rencontres avec Péguy*, pp. 189–223.

VIGNEAULT, ROBERT. "Un univers interdit" in Simone Fraisse, ed., *Les critiques de notre temps et Péguy*, pp. 145–59.

WILSON, NELLY. "A Contribution to the Study of Péguy's Anti-intellectualism: Early Revolt against the Spirit of the Sorbonne," *Symposium*, no. 1 (Spring, 1966). pp. 63–78.

WINLING, RAYMOND. "Péguy-Nietzsche: Un chrétien du Parvis répond à l'auteur de Zarathoustra," *Revue des Sciences Religieuses*, no. 3 (July 1972), pp. 212–55.

ZOPPI, GILBERT. "Péguy et Molière," *Australian Journal of French Studies*, no. 1 (January-April 1973), pp. 32–41.

Index

Aeschylus, 64, 99, 127
Agamemnon, 114
Alexander I (of Yugoslavia), 75
Alexander the Great, 65, 114
Allemane, Jean, 48
Allier, Raoul, 45
Andler, Charles, 80
Apollinaire, Guillaume, 20, 125
Aristotle, 114
Avenard, Etienne, 47

Babut, Charles, 81
Balzac, Honoré de, 124
Barrès, Maurice, 19, 72, 128
Barthou, Louis, 75
Baudelaire, Charles, 109, 150
Baudin, Alphonse, 59
Baudouin, Marcel, 17, 23, 88, 93
Beaumarchais, Pierre Augustin Caron
  de, 62, 135
Bédier, Joseph, 81
Beethoven, Ludwig van, 132
Bellais, Georges, 18
Benda, Julien, 19, 22, 83, 85, 128
Béranger, Pierre Jean de, 112
Bergson, Henri, 23, 35-36, 83-86,
  141
Bichet, René, 106
Bloch, Gustave, 62
Blum, Léon, 18, 34, 35, 65
Boitier, Louis, 35
Bossuet, Jacques-Bénigne, 34
Boudon, Victor, 17
Boulanger, General Georges, 27
Bourgeois, André, 74
Brasillach, Robert, 149
Brunetière, Ferdinand, 31, 34, 80-81
Butor, Michel, 63, 89, 115

Caesar, Julius, 116
Calvin, John, 85
Camus, Albert, 62
Casimir-Périer, Claude, 22
Casimir-Périer, Simone, 22
Cervantes Saavedra, Miguel de, 84
Charlemagne, 116
Charles X, 116
Chateaubriand, François-René de,
  148
Cheops, 116
Claudel, Paul, 147
Colette, Gabrielle, 147
Columbus, Christopher, 85
Combes, Emile, 60, 62, 65
Corneille, Pierre, 47, 71, 80, 84-87,
  116, 131-34, 138, 145
Cruppi, Mme, 75

Dagobert I, 92
Dante Alighieri, 84
Darius the Great, 114
David (King), 116
Descartes, René, 83, 84-85
Desjardins, Paul, 49
Doumer, Paul, 93
Dreyfus, Alfred, 16, 17, 18, 38, 69
Dreyfus Affair (Dreyfusism, Drey-
  fusite), 17-18, 20-21, 28, 30, 31,
  32, 33, 34, 35, 38, 40, 42, 43,
  46, 50, 57, 59, 60, 63, 68, 69-70,
  78, 81, 82, 93, 132, 140, 141, 144
Dumas fils, Alexandre, 116
Durkheim, Emile, 62, 81

Einstein, Albert, 50, 144
Esterhazy, Charles Marie Ferdinand
  Walsen-, 34

Euripides, 127
Evrard, Guillaume, 90

Favre, Geneviève, 100
Fénelon, François de Salignac de La
   Mothe-, 50
Ferry, Jules, 85
Flaubert, Gustave, 44
Fournier, Henri, 22
France, Anatole, 19, 29, 61, 130
Franklin, Benjamin, 86
Freud, Sigmund, 50

Gallieni, General Joseph, 45
Galliffet, General Gaston de, 57
Gide, André, 20, 147
Goethe, Johann Wolfgang von, 84
Grasset, Bernard, 22, 74
Guesde, Jules, 27, 35, 38
Guieysse, Charles, 37-38

Hadrian, 65
Halévy, Daniel, 19, 66-68, 69, 70-
   73, 130
Halévy, Ludovic, 73
Hercules, 114
Herod the Great, 98
Herodotus, 114
Herr, Lucien, 18, 20, 27, 32, 33,
   34, 81
Hervé, Gustave, 68, 69, 82
Hesiod, 64
Homer, 62, 63, 64, 84, 99, 127
Hugo, Victor, 31, 46, 47, 62, 64,
   71-72, 83-86, 112, 115, 116, 134-
   37, 142

Jaurès, Jean, 19, 20, 22, 26, 28, 29,
   32, 33, 36, 38, 40, 42, 47, 48, 62,
   68, 69, 71, 78-79, 81, 82, 85
Jesus Christ, 65, 94, 96, 109
Joan of Arc, 17, 70, 76, 77, 80, 86,
   97, 101, 103, 110, 149, 150
Joinville, Jean de, 70, 77, 97
Joseph, 97

Kahn, Gustave, 142

Lafargue, Paul, 38, 48
Lamartine, Alphonse de, 47, 116
Langlois, Charles-Victor, 62, 79-81
Lannes, Marshal Jean, 59
Lanson, Gustave, 56, 62, 77, 80-82,
   116, 130
Lantier, Cyprien, 31
Laudet, Fernand, 75, 78, 79, 130
Laurens, Pierre, 74-75
Lavergne, Antonin, 40-41
Lavisse, Ernest, 62, 75, 77, 79, 80-
   81, 116-17
Lazare, Bernard, 59, 68, 77
Leconte de Lisle, Charles-Marie, 48,
   135
Le Grix, François, 75-76
Lotte, Joseph, 21, 104
Louis-Philippe, 116

Mallarmé, Stéphane, 150
Mangasarian, M., 43
Maritain, Jacques, 21, 100
Marix, Eddy, 59
Marx, Karl, 38
Mercier, General Auguste, 38
Michelet, Jules, 31, 36, 50, 76, 89,
   132, 135, 146
Milliet, Paul (The Milliets), 66
Molière (Jean-Baptiste Poquelin),
   87, 102, 129, 131-32
Monet, Claude, 62, 64
Moréas, Jean, 128
Mounet-Sully (Jean Sully Mounet),
   16

Napoleon I, 46, 59, 116
Naudy, Théodore, 78

Pascal, Blaise, 26, 27, 28-29, 39, 48,
   128-31
Péguy, Cécile Quéré (mother), 15,
   23
Péguy, Charles:

WORKS: POETRY
   A Domremy, 88-89, 119-21
   "Aveugle, L'," 99
   Ballade du coeur, La, 22, 116
   "Banlieue, La," 99-100

Batailles, Les, 88-89

Chanson du roi Dagobert, La, 19, 21, 92-93

"Châteaux de Loire," 99

"Epave, L'," 98-99

Eve, 23, 59, 95, *109-15,* 116, 125, 135

Jeanne d'Arc, 17, 21, *88-92,* 93, 116, 119

Mystère de la charité de Jeanne d'Arc, Le, 22, 75-76, *93-95,* 116, 123

Mystère des saints innocents, Le, 23, 70, 97-98

OEuvres choisies 1900-1910, 22, 84

"Paris," 99

"Paris double galère," 105

"Paris vaisseau de charge," 104

"Paris vaisseau de guerre," 105

Porche du mystère de la deuxième vertu, Le, 95-96, 123-24

Premier Livre des ballades, 116

"Présentation de la Beauce à Notre Dame de Chartres," *105-107,* 108, 124-25

"Présentation de Paris à Notre Dame," 104

"Prière de confidence," 108

"Prière de déférence," *108-109,* 124-25

"Prière de demande," 107-108

"Prière de report," 108

"Prière de résidence," 107

Quatrains, 22, *116-17*

Rouen, 88-91, 121-23

"Sainte Geneviève patronne de Paris," 100

"Sept contre Paris, Les," *99-100,* 116

"Sept contre Thèbes, Les," 99

Tapisserie de Notre Dame, La, 96, *104-107*

Tapisserie de sainte Geneviève et de Jeanne d'Arc, La, 23, *100-103*

"Urne, L'," 98-99

WORKS: PROSE

"Amis des Cahiers, Les," 74

"A nos amis, à nos abonnés," *58-59,* 74, 112

"Argent, L'," 61, *78-80,* 149

"Argent suite, L'," 80-82

"Avertissement," 43-44

"Brève réponse à Jaurès," 29-31

"Cahiers de la Quinzaine," 49

"Casse-cou," 33-34

"Clio, dialogue de l'histoire et de l'âme païenne," 61-64

"Compte rendu de congrès," 35-36

"Compte rendu de mandat," 34-35

"Courrier de Russie," 47

"Débats parlementaires," 42

"De Jean Coste," *40-41,* 60, 70, 72

"De la cité socialiste," 25, 138, 147

"De la grippe," *27-28*

"De la raison," 36-37

"De la situation faite à l'histoire et à la sociologie dans les temps modernes," *49-50,* 68

"De la situation faite à l'histoire et à la sociologie et de la situation faite au parti intellectuel dans le monde moderne," 55

"De la situation faite au parti intellectuel dans le monde moderne," 50-54

"De la situation faite au parti intellectuel dans le monde moderne devant les accidents de la gloire temporelle," 55-57

"Délation aux droits de l'homme, La," 46

"Elections, Les," 40

"Encore de la grippe," 27, 28

"Essai de monopole, Un," 45-46

"Il me plaît . . . ," 75

"Lettre à M. Charles Guieysse," 37-38

"Lettre du provincial," 26, 128

"Louis de Gonzague," *48-49,* 130

"Marcel, premier dialogue de la cité harmonieuse," 25-26

"Note conjointe sur M. Descartes et la philosophie cartésienne," 84-87
"Note conjointe sur Victor Hugo," 84
"Note sur M. Bergson et la philosophie bergsonienne," 83-84
"Notre Jeunesse," 66-71
"Notre Patrie," 46-47
"Nous devons nous préparer . . . ," 39
"Nous sommes des vaincus," 60-61, 72, 74
"Nouveau théologien, Un," 75-78, 130-31
"OEuvres choisies de Charles Péguy 1900-1910," 74-75
"Orléans vu de Montargis," 44
"Personnalités," 38
"Pour ma maison," 31-32
"Pour moi," 32
"Reprise politique parlementaire," 42-43, 70
"Suppliants parallèles, Les," 47, 126-27
"Toujours de la grippe," 27, 28-29, 118-19, 129
" 'Triomphe de la République,' Le," 26-27
"Véronique, dialogue de l'histoire et de l'âme charnelle," 64-66
"Victor-Marie, comte Hugo," 71-73, 74, 75, 76, 77
"Vraiment vrai," 36
"Zangwill," 44-45

Péguy, Charlotte Baudouin (wife), 17, 18, 21, 22
Péguy, Désiré (father), 15
Péguy, Germaine (daughter), 20
Péguy, Marcel (son), 17, 18, 99
Péguy, Pierre (son), 21, 23
Pelletan, Camille, 62
Peslöüan, Charles-Lucas de, 74-75
Peter the Great, 65
Pindar, 64
Planck, Max, 50

Plato, 55, 114
Porché, François, 19, 47
Pressensé, Francis de, 48, 82
Proust, Marcel, 29, 57, 80, 147
Prudentius, 98
Psichari, Ernest, 72

Quéré, Etiennette (grandmother), 15, 92
Quicherat, Jules, 76, 89

Rabelais, François, 89, 115
Racine, Jean, 29, 37, 71, 129, 131-33, 138
Raphaël, Blanche, 21, 22
Reinach, Joseph, 57
Rembrandt van Rijn, 132
Renan, Ernest, 28, 29, 37, 39, 44, 50, 51, 55, 72, 116, 137-40
Rimbaud, Arthur, 25
Roland, Lucien, 35
Rolland, Romain, 19, 22, 49, 61, 85, 145-46
Roque, Mario, 18
Rudler, G., 80, 130

St. Eloi, 92-93
St. Geneviève, 100-101, 103, 110
St. George, 89
St. John, 77
St. Louis (Louis IX), 70, 77, 86, 97
St. Louis de Gonzague, 48-49, 130
St. Luke, 77, 96
St. Mark, 77
St. Mary, 96, 97, 110, 116
St. Matthew, 65, 77, 98
St. Michael, 89
Sartre, Jean-Paul, 66, 78
Scheurer-Kestner, Auguste, 93
Schwarzkoppen, Maximilian von, 34
Seignobos, Charles, 62, 81-82
Shakespeare, William, 84, 96, 133, 134
Solomon (King), 131
Sophocles, 16, 29, 48, 89, 126-28
Suarès, André, 19
Sully-Prudhomme (René-François-Armand Prudhomme), 31

Taine, Hippolyte, 44-45, 55, 116, 137, *139-40*
Tharaud, Jérôme and Jean, 19, 49
Theseus, 114
Tolstoy, Leo, 31, 134

Umberto I, 93

Vaillant, Edouard, 33, 35, 38, 48
Valéry, Paul, 147
Verlaine, Paul, 102
Vigny, Alfred de, 31, 47, 92

Villon, François, 47
Viviani, René, 51
Voltaire (François-Marie Arouet), 148

Wallon, Henri, 89
Walras, Léon, 17
William II (of Germany), 21

Zangwill, Israël, 44
Zeno, 114
Zola, Emile, 17, 31, 130, *140-44*